T0368685

In The Beginning

SHIRLEY SHEPPARD

authorHOUSE®

AuthorHouse™
1663 Liberty Drive
Bloomington, IN 47403
www.authorhouse.com
Phone: 1-800-839-8640

First published by AuthorHouse 03/16/2011

ISBN: 978-1-4567-4999-6 (ebk)
ISBN: 978-1-4567-1083-5 (sc)

Printed in the United States of America

Any people depicted in stock imagery provided by Thinkstock are models, and such images are being used for illustrative purposes only.
Certain stock imagery © Thinkstock.

This book is printed on acid-free paper.

I want to give thanks to the Lord Jesus for my daughter Beckie Sheppard Who has been a blessing to me in her prayers and devotion in my life. She Has encouraged me to puplish my book. My granddaughter Kalisha Daniel Who also has always believed in me with support as well as prayers.

To
Albert Joseph,
My Dad,
Who has gone
To be with
The Lord.

Acknowledgement

There are many people who have contributed to this book. As space does not allow listing all their names, some will have to be omitted. I want to say "thank you!" to them as well as to:

My four daughters. They have all been supportive of me and of this ministry. Each one is appreciated more than I can say. All stay in close contact and bless me through their love, which is shown in many different ways. May the Lord bless each of you, and draw you ever closer to Himself.

My stepmother, Josephine Joseph, who cared for and loved that motherless child. Through all the years, she has never failed me.

My mother in the Lord, Geraldine McDaniels, whose book, *God is the Answer*, led me to Him as Saviour. Without that step, this story could not have been written.

My dear sister in Christ, Toni Young, who held me in prayer during the darkest moments.

My father in the Gospel, Reverend Charles Stillwell and his wife Bobbie. They have blessed me often and in so many concrete ways!

Many sisters and brothers in Chrit across these United States, wherever you are, I thank God for each one. You have faithfully been interceding when only the Lord knew how badly I needed those prayers!

Nevada Strode, who put it all together, and her husband Jay. Their peaceful home Cosecha Ranch, has been a haven where I could rest and write. They prayed for, and believed in, this Evangelist doing what God had said to do. When He told me to write this book, Nevada said I could. I wasn't all that sure! As with everything in my life, Jesus was there to help, for He is "The Only Way."

Table of Contents

1

In the Beginning

Over and over I told thoe two white women, "Mama just went to the store! She'll be right back, honest!" Of course, I knew Mama wasn't coming "right back." There was no telling when, or if, she would return.

While gathering up our things, they said little. I heard the taller one murmur, "Rare for a black woman to leave her kids."

The other said something about, "Biggest 'un took good care of them others . . . for three days!"

At seven, I was oldest, and Albert next. We were thin, with dark brown hair and eyes like Dad. My baby sister, Loretta, was less than a year. Diane had come between her and Albert, but she didn't live with us. When she was born, Mama's mother fell in love with her. Dad allowed Grandma Roderick to take her, but regretted it later. Mama's behavior was so erratic, he probably thought two children were enough. Loretta was chubby, but pretty, like Mama.

Wide-eyed Albert stood watching those two black-clad women go through our home. As Mama always left me in charge when she went away, he didn't understand what was going on.

Those women were frightening me, because they might be police. Our mother had always warned, when leaving us, "Shirley, don't let anybody know you kids are alone or the police will come and take you all away." That threat had hung over us as long as I could remember. They didn't look like police, but maybe . . .

1

That time we had been alone three endless days and nights. Dad came home after work as sure as the sun rose over the Atlantic. His coming was always the high point of my day. It wasn't unusual for Mama to be gone, but he was the rock to which we clung.

While alone, caring for the little ones, panic had twisted my insides. Something terrible must have happened to our father. I knew it down deep. Dad would come if he could . . .

The two women had said almost nothing while going through our stuff. Silence made things worse. When Albert whispered, "Why don't ya' stop 'em, Shirley?" I felt both betrayed and betrayer.

Even when home from her mysterious trips, Mama had always made me responsible for the little ones. So they hadn't been alarmed at all by our being alone. I, however, was eaten up by anxiety for Dad. Thinking the police might come and take us away had added to the terror. It had been a heavy load, but those women taking control was even more frightening. Seeing myself as a failure, I wondered. What would Mama say?

Each of those three days the kids were fed, but thinking about Dad brought cramps 'till food would not go down. The others were too little to share my worries. Thoughts had flown around in my head like birds; Dad could not know we were alone! He would never leave us like that Something really bad must have happened!

Mama's absence was to be expected. But Dad's was worrisome. He must need help, but what could I do? Fright kept washing over me like waves of the ocean.

Because of Mama's strange disappearances, our parents had quarreled a lot. Nevertheless, Dad loved his family, and was really good to us. I had never understood why his beautiful wife could not cope with life.

Now I realize that immaturity was part of the problem. Married at sixteen, she'd had four children by Caesarian Section. That trauma would have added to the depression and her other problems. Why our mother left, or where she went, was a mystery. It still is.

Suddenly one of the strangers took my arm. "No! No!" I begged. "Don't take us away. Dad won't know where we are!"

As the tall one pulled me toward the door, my terror grew out of control. "Mama's at the store!" I screamed. Long legs kicking at her shins, I clutched the door frame. "She'll be right back, honest!"

I had been telling neighbors that for years. Why wouldn't those scarey women believe me? Why didn't Dad come? Mama wouldn't care, but he'd be heartbroken to find us gone. I battled those women. As kicking didn't help, I hit them with both fists.

One pushed and the other tugged to force me out of the house. Fright raised my voice to a shriek, "Don't you see? Dad won't know where we are!" Neither replied. Though I kicked a bit and clawed it accomplished nothing. I could not live up to the task Mama had given me!

My brother, sister, and I were none too gently put into a car and driven off. Albert and Loretta were sobbing. They didn't understand and were probably frightened as much by my behavior as by the strangers.

Today it is plain the Lord was there all the time. How impossible that a seven-year old could take care of herself and two other children for that long! It was God who arranged for us to be rescued, horrible as it seemed at the time. When neighbors reported our situation to a church, those two ladies came. Probably hatred of the job explained their silence.

I had always taken very seriously the responsibility of caring for Albert and Loretta. Because of that, a heavy sense of failure was added to my fright. When the two women first appeared, I had said to Albert, "If only Dad comes, everything will be all right." Beyond any shadow of doubting, I knew he wouldn't allow them to take us. It seemed they were stealing us, instead of helping. Where could he be?

We were taken to O'Rourke's Childrens' Center in Providence, Rhode Island, which was run by the state Welfare Department. Mama neither called nor did she come. That wasn't surprising. But not hearing from Dad really scared me. Something terrible must have happened. None of our family ever came, to say where he was, or to explain.

It is impossible for people who never were abandoned to comprehend that feeling. We seemed utterly lost, throwaways. Much of the time, I felt as if somebody was choking me. At others it seemed I was drowning and nobody in the world cared.

O'Rourke childrens' Center was no movie set for Hollywood's idea of an orphanage! Made up of ten or fifteen cottages, each had a kitchen, living room, and bath. Every cottage had seven or eight bedrooms, which were shared by two children. These were neat and roomy. We had radios, games, and toys for entertainment – but oh the days seemed long! I, too proud to cry in front of the other kids, put up a front. The adults at the Center, all white, showed no compassion, and I burned with anger toward them. Tears soaked my

3

pillow night after night, but few people ever saw me cry. Lonely and filled with despair, I had nowhere to turn. Except to God, whom I didn't really know!

The other children there told hideous tales about orphanages and cruelty they had experienced. We didn't' know what to believe or what not to. Some knew their parents were dead. Others, abandoned like us, had no idea why they were there. None of us knew how long we might have to stay. Questions chased each other through my mind, but answers never followed.

Rarely did Albert and I have a minute alone. Occasionally he would sidle up to me in the crowd, whispering, "the other kids say we're orphans. That we'll be here forever. It ain't true, is it, Shirley?"

Feeling a total failure, I could only put my arms around him and say, not believing a word of it, "'Course not. We're not like those others. We have a family!"

Harder questions follows. "Where's Mama? She's always come home before! And what about Dad?"

With everything in me, I wanted to trust our father. Yet doubts whispered inside my head. It had always been easy for Mama to forsake us. Would a man be so different?

Albert's huge brown eyes demanded an answer. I was forced to say, "Dad will come, you know he always has." But doubts chewed away. Where was he? Would we ever see him again?

I covered up my head with a pillow at night, but those thoughts wouldn't stop. If he really loved us, surely there'd be some word. In the dark, a most horrible thought would sneak up on me. Maybe he was dead! The only relief was sleep. Though tardy, it always came.

The Center's staff kept us apart as much as possible. When we did catch a moment together, Albert asked one day, "Why doesn't Grandma Joseph come?" As Dad's mother had always been special to us, I wondered that myself. There were questions, questions, but no answers.

I tried to be grown up, "Things'll get better. They have to!"

Like me, he never cried in front of others. "But, Shirley," he asked, and I knew tears were near the surface, "Where's our aunts and uncles? Doesn't somebody love us anymore?"

My own situation was impossible, but knowing that he needed comforting made me feel even worse. Every time I thought of Albert and Loretta, something inside me shriveled. She had always been "mine." It seemed impossible for her to adjust to the Center as other babies did. When she saw me and cried, I really wanted to die. It seemed the whole world had fallen apart. Hopelessness grew inside me like a huge cancer.

Looking back, I realize that Jesus, who loves us so much, loved me then, and I praise His Name. Surely it all happened for a reason. My enormous love for children, especially those without parents, may have been planted then. Jesus was there, even in our misery. He never fails to look after children, but I didn't know Him personally as I do now.

Weeks passed and nobody contacted us. Forty years later Dad's sister finally explained, "Your father was ill and in a coma for days." I asked why he never came to visit us. "He spent several weeks in the hospital afterward, very, very ill. The doctors feared a relapse if he learned about the predicament you children were in."

"But Dad must have missed us!" I exclaimed. "Didn't he ask any questions?"

"The family decided to keep him in the dark," she said, "and all efforts to find your mother were fruitless."

As have been my own, though I anticipate meeting her eventually. Having seen miracle after miracle, I know nothing is beyond God. She has been in my prayers through all the years, and I expect Him to be faithful! Of course, Mama's relatives had no way of knowing about our desperate situation. They didn't even know she was gone again.

Dad's people were Portuguese. His was a large and very close family. But they kept their own counsel. His mother, Mary Joseph, did not speak English well. Perhaps because of that, she didn't contact the Center about us.

During long, lonely hours, I could picture her, tall, light complected with red hair and brown eyes. Her house was always such a happy place. Dad's father, her first husband, and several sons had been merchant seamen.

Her second husband, Manuel, also had a large family, so when both groups came together their house was filled. One uncle played the piano and my father the violin. Forlorn, in the Center, I used to picture them all dancing to their Portuguese music. It seemed they were in another world. Of course that made our situation the more hideous.

"Won't we see any of them ever again?" I would ask that tear-soaked pillow. "I'll be good, and never sass Mama again, if only Dad will come and take us home." It seemed I must have done something evil to deserve such terrible punishment.

As my father and I had always been very close, losing him was unbelievably painful. I had often seen him cry, when Mother was away on one of her trips. He would murmur, "What am I to do?" the picture is still very clear – that dark head down on the table, and his tears.

Upset, I would console him, "don't worry, Dad, I'll take care of you and the kids."

His Uncle Albert, who was Pentecostal, had always influenced me greatly. The other kids, thinking him too religious and kind of peculiar, always ran away when he came. I was different, and loved being with that great uncle. He often took time to talk and to pray with me.

Even as a little girl, something inside me always had said there was a God. At the State Home, aching with lonliness, I never doubted that He was someplace, listening, and that He cared about us. It seemed He must hate our miserable circumstances. Too. Because of that, I often prayed, "Oh, God, get us out of here. Please take us back. Make us a family again!"

The Center's staff made it almost impossible for me to comfort my sister and brother, though I tried. There were only a few black children and the matrons were very prejudiced. How I hate them!

Night after night I begged God, "Bring somebody who loves us to visit." I felt more desolate every day. "You know I can't help the little ones. Everybody hates us and this place is so awful!" Only His Grace kept me free of bitterness toward the white race. His Hand was on my life even then!

Eventually God answered those prayers, and Dad came. How many months later, I don't know. Each one had seemed a year. Oh the joy! The boundless joy of seeing that handsome man! Albert Joseph was not quite six feet, strong and muscular. He had a magnificent personality. Like Albert's, his brown eyes were very expressive.

After several visits, he came one day with bad news. My brother and I were leaning on his knees, Loretta on his lap. "I can't take you out of here," he told us, sorrowfully, "because there's nobody at home to take care of kids."

Immediately I began to argue, "But I always took good care of the others!"

"Shirley," he tried to explain, "the authorities won't allow you to leave under those conditions."

It was a terrible blow. "I'll visit as often as possible." Dad said, trying to help us understand. My brother was sobbing, he loved our father as much as I did. "Son, please believe this is hard on me, too! I'll get you out," Dad promised, tears in his own eyes, "as soon as there's a way!" I, who had never stopped praying for and expecting God's help, was devastated.

Though Dad brought us clothes, toys, and goodies every visit, we all felt unloved and forgotten. "Things" cannot replace a parent's attention and affection. I should have learned that then, but made those same mistakes as a mother many years later. It hurts even today to realize my daughters often felt that same pain. I gave them "things" instead of time and attention.

Life improved some when we were placed in a foster home. Dad could then visit us three or four times a week, but my heart sobbed every time he left. It seemed cruel that we had to be separated, and impossible to understand.

Years later Dad shared with me how painful that time was for him. I didn't realize that he was asking God for help, also. Praying for a wife so we could be a family again, he thought several times God was answering. However those women were scared off by us children. Mothering three so young must have seemed a formidable task.

Then God answered! He brought us a very special lady. Josephine was so full of love, I liked her from the first moment I saw her. About five and a half feet tall, with pretty dark brown hair and eyes, she was really attractive. Stepmothers are joked about, often unkindly, but ours brought such joy! Even before their marriage, she filled that awful hole in our lives.

Josephine, with great wisdom, wanted us to get acquainted quickly. She knew that would be easier on everybody later. Often we were taken on picnics, to the movies, or out to eat! What Heaven it was! It seemed I had been motherless forever. That lovely woman really wanted to be with me! Words cannot express what Josephine has meant to me through the years. I saw her then, and do now, as a gift from the very Hand of God!

After Dad's marriage, we moved to Rochester, Massachusetts. It was his new wife's birthplace and many of her relatives lived in that little country town. They were a close family like Dad's had always been. Sharing whatever they had, each believed in helping the other. We kids weren't enthused about leaving the city, but knew it had to beat that foster home. We all moved into Josephine's house and slept in comfortable beds for a change. She was a comforting sort of person. A true home maker, she was generous and loved sharing with others.

I especially appreciated her taste in clothes. At Children's Center, uniforms were a must and how we hated them! The food was terrible, and didn't improve much at the foster home. The "mother" there gave her grandchildren and husband the best. They saved money on what we foster children ate. Josephine was an excellent cook and did we eat! Basking in a wonderful new security, we soon learned to call her "Mom." Our days in the Center had been stark, empty of love and laughter. Suddenly life was full to the brim, full of all that makes it worthwhile.

2

Heaven Is a Family

We worked hard in the country, but were delighted to be away from all those strangers. Dad worked in construction, so was gone much of the time. We missed him, but Mom's garden, chickens and other things connected with rural life kept us busy.

The house had ten rooms but Josephine's mother lived on the first floor. Upstairs there were three bedrooms, a living room and small kitchen, which met our needs nicely. The bathroom was outside, which seemed queer to city kids.

Ocean Spray Cranberry Company was across the street. From time to time our parents and other relatives were employed there. It was hard, working in the cranberry bogs. Our house was about fifteen miles from Onset Beach, at Onset, Massachusetts. We often visited there.

Dad's family, as well as Mama's, were seamen. Grandfather Joseph had captained a ship on the Atlantic Ocean. He and my grandmother came from Cape Verde Islands, off the coast of Africa. When they moved to East Providence he continued going to sea. Grandmother used to tell us, "I begged your grandfather not to take our youngest son on that voyage, but he felt the boy was old enough to go." She would say, tears in her eyes, "their ship went down, and all aboard were lost.

Salt water must have run in Dad's veins because of his seafaring family. He loved the ocean and was an excellent swimmer. I, too, loved the water, but not swimming. I was thrown in as a child, supposedly to teach me. It didn't work, and that is not a wise move. I never did learn.

My favorite occupation was walking along the shore. Having my feet in the sand gave me a freedom found nowhere else. For some reason I often felt burdened. The water and sand could erase that feeling. God always seemed nearer then, and I felt protected in an inexplicable way.

Dad loved the outdoors, so there were many cook-outs while we were growing up. Josephine and he took us on all-day picnics where there was band music and plenty of food. The best part, when Mom's relatives came, was having everybody together. After those traumatic months at the State Home, abandoned, family reunions were always a joy to my soul. When it was time to leave, Dad often asked me to find Loretta and Albert. Usually they then would be unable to find me, which aggravated him.

"I'll never take you anywhere again," he would exclaim, acting cross. We were so much alike, he knew I hated to leave. None of us were ever deprived of those outings as punishment. Our parents knew how much family meant to us, so we did many things together.

There were Chinese restaurants in the area and all of us loved that food. After eating, we would go to a movie. Dad especially like cowboy and Indian pictures. Mom usually fell asleep and he would threaten, "You'll have to stay home next time!" never meaning a word of it.

Our parents did not believe in leaving children home as so many do today. I believe there is nothing like a family spending time together, whether to worship or to have fun. There is so much lonliness in the world, often because of broken families. Doing more things together might help that situation. Too many parents want to entertain themselves – golfing, bowling, or wating TV – instead of doing things as a family. Dad and Mom gave of their time and affection freely. There was a commitment to their children often absent today.

Our new mother was Catholic and very religious, so each Sunday the family attended mass. We children went to catechism class once a week, to be taught Catholic theology by the nuns. I never liked them much because most of them appeared heartless. They didn't seem to love anybody – even little children. Discipline was their thing, and this can damage a child when it is not mixed with affection.

We knew about harsh discipline. In the foster and state homes, love was almost nonexistent. That was especially true for black children. There was heavy prejudice. It often showed through unfair punishment and cruelty in the name of discipline.

The Lord wants children to behave, and expects adults to live disciplined lives also. Yet He never deprives us of love, no matter how bad we are. It is available, no matter what! John 3:16, KJV, says, "For God so loved the world that He gave His only begotten Son that whosoever (includes you and me) shall believe in Him shall not perish, but have everlasting life." Truly that kind of Love is the answer for hurting people everywhere.

It seemed there was always a yearning for genuine love in my heart. Though our parents loved us, I felt there was something missing. Today, knowing that only genuine love is God's kind, I realize that emptiness was my heart pining for Jesus Christ. Once He is invited in, Jesus can doctor hurts, no matter what caused them. His Love sews up wounds in us as nothing else can. Paul says in Hebrews 13:8, "Jesus Christ is the same yesterday, today and forever." We cannot say that about mortals, no matter how good they seem!

At times I have been misunderstood, brokenhearted, and misused. Friends have turned away and relatives failed to understand. Through it all I learned Jesus is 100 percent trustworthy. More than a friend, He is never too tired to listen. When we take problems to Him, Jesus is never "too busy." Our Lord is available round the clock. The promise "I will never leave thee, nor forsake thee" is from one who cannot lie! (Hebrews 13:5). Jesus loves us even when we make mistakes and picks us up if we stumble. We need only ask! Things in my life that looked impossible were surmounted because He loved and helped me through them.

When the goodness of Jesus Christ comes to mind, my soul leaps for joy. We don't give Him enough praise for His goodness and mercy toward us. Too much time is spent complaining or giving the devil credit. Jesus Christ is faithful to do what He has promised. Human minds find that difficult to fathom because people so often fail us.

Because of the responsibility placed on me at home in Rochester, I was mature for my age. Things most children enjoy were never for me. Mom had turned me into a good housekeeper and fair cook, by the age of twelve. Still trying to mother the other children, I just was not appreciated by them!

As our village was far out in the country and had few teenagers, my parents allowed me to move to Wareham, Massachusetts, for high school. Mom's sister lived there and Wareham High wasn't far from her house. It was wonderful having boys and girls my age nearby.

Aunt Lena was kind and we got along well. I helped her with her two children and did whatever she asked. I often baby-sat after school and during vacations. The money was needed for school clothes. Josephine held it for me and was so good about helping me, if there wasn't enough.

When I was eighteen I left Aunt Lena's home to live with Mary Roderick. She was my real mother's mother. Before Mama left us, our family had enjoyed many good times at her home in East Providence, Rhode Island. Short, with long straight black hair, she could tell the funniest stories about life in Portugal. Black eyes sparkling, Grandma loved to reminisce about earlier times in the "old country."

Grandmother Roderick was a fantastic cook. She had been chief baker in some restaurant for many years. I can almost taste her delicious home made pies and cakes after all the years. Her speciality was fancy pastry and we kids loved those cream puffs and éclairs. Her husband was a chef at the same restaurant. He had grapes in the yard and made wine out of them. Morally, they were good people, but they never attended any church.

The Bible teaches salvation comes only through accepting the sacrifice of Jesus Christ dying on the Cross for each of us individually. Being good never saved anyone! My prayer is that both of them found Him as Savior before they died.

After Grandfather Roderick's death, his wife became diabetic. When I lived there she was quite ill and unable to work. One foot had been amputated and the other one was being affected. My sister Diane still lived with her as did two older cousins. Diane was small and still looked very much like our mother. A beautiful girl, she had inherited Grandmother's sense of humor and was always fun to be around.

The four-room house was crowded and Grandmother's welfare check stretched to its limit. Dad tried to buy Diane's clothes, and to give Grandmother money so we could eat. As she didn't get much financial support for keeping the two cousins, they found jobs selling newspapers and working at the bowling alley. The economy was bad, and money scarce, so they wisely decided to join the Air Force. Both saved every dollar possible toward buying Grandmother a home. Unfortunately, her death robbed them of that blessing.

Before they left, I told her, "Grandmother, your load is heavy enough. I am going to move in with Anna Cabral, my Godmother, and lighten it a bit." Though hating to see me go, Grandmother understood.

I had always loved Anna, who also lived in Providence. Divorced, with three young sons, she needed help, so I received a warm welcome. She was a sweet, loving person, who had the most beautiful dark brown eyes. My godmother was always helping people. Cooking food for the sick or hungry and delivering it was her way of life. She genuinely cared about others, and was especially good to me.

When I was eighteen my Godmother and her sons built a house. She could do anything. I particularly remember her as an excellent seamstress, making dresses and suits for both men and women, as well as draperies and car seats. It seemed nothing was too difficult for her to sew. She lives in that house yet, and enjoys the boys and their families who live nearby.

I soon found a job and made it a point to visit Grandmother Roderick often. She was always glad to see me, for we loved one another. I cleaned the house and bought what groceries I could afford, Diane was about twelve and needed so many things, and I helped out as much as possible. Though poverty always growled at the door, it was a happy home. Everybody loved my Grandmother.

Sugar diabetes took her life at only sixty-two. It was my privilege to be with her at the end, but because she was in a coma, she never knew it. The years of mama's absence had taken their toll. Grandmother, troubled that they might never be together again, talked about her a lot before that last illness. Anyone whose child has disappeared knows the sorrow and its pain. She suffered emotionally as well as physically!

Though I continue believing Mother is alive, and that one day we will meet, only God can bring it about. Not knowing whether a loved one is alive or dead means constant anxiety, unless we are leaning on Jesus. I praise God for taking all of that burden from me. Perhaps Grandmother would have lived longer had she known Him and His peace.

After graduating from high school, I felt quite grown up and able to manage my own life. Up to then I had been sheltered, with loving relatives and friends on all sides. With no idea how cruel people could be, I expected to be treated kindly, no matter what the future held.

With horror I found there are some who enjoy brutally punishing others, for whatever reason strikes their fancy. Little did I know what life in that jungle was like. It came near being my death.

3

From Misery to Misery

While I was visiting a friend in Providence, a handsome merchant seaman crossed my path. Perhaps that seafaring blood in our veins was to blame for his appeal. Not only Dad's family, but Mother's, too, worked on ships.

For whatever reason, I was attracted to the seaman. Perhaps those old stories of the sea were to blame for his appeal. Not only Dad's family, but Mother's, too, worked on ships.

For whatever reason, I was attracted to the seaman. Perhaps those old stories of the sea were to blame. "Love at first sight" sees only what it wants to see. And hears that it wants to hear! One of my cousins, also nineteen, wasn't as naïve as I. "Shirley," she asked, "can't you see the guy is a typical sailor?"

I, searching for someone to love who would love me in return, replied, "Oh, no, he is wonderful!"

"Every time you need that guy, he will be at sea!" she said, with expression, "Those kind love their ships more than their wives!"

"He's a sharp dresser," I retorted, "and I like that in a man."

She really tried, but I heard his soft talk, and nothing else. "Love" came in and chased my common sense right out the window!

My parents tried to warn me, and did not give their permission for the marriage. Dad had always anticipated giving me away at a church wedding. To this day I regret hurting them, but so often young people walk in pure selfishness!

We met in July and were married in October. Expecting pure bliss, I walked into a horror movie and Shirley was the star. Words cannot describe the abuse I suffered. My daughter, Lu'anna, is the only good thing which came from that union.

When she was ten months old I left her father and went to live with my father. He and Mom were very supportive and insisted we stay with them indefinitely. Because of the marriage and its torture, I was ill and a nervous wreck. After being kicked in the stomach, I had miscarried a baby boy.

Totally disillusioned, I felt not only rejected – but worthless. At twenty-one, I couldn't sleep and when I ate I became nauseated. My hair was falling out and my weight was down. Any noise at night terrified me. Oh, that awful fear! It was only the grace of God which kept me from a nervous breakdown.

My stepmother's kindness will never be forgotten. She helped me back to normal by purchasing vitamins. Insisting that I take them, Mom also cooked what I needed. I had lived at near starvation level for so long, coming back to myself was a slow process.

So much trauma in that nightmare marriage had affected Lu'anna. Even after we were safe at home, she cried a lot, didn't eat, and was frail. Dad often sang and played his violin to calm her, and to make her smile. Probably it was my own nervousness that made her cranky, but neither of us could sleep.

Too sick to work, I was forced to accept my parents' hospitality. It was difficult, after not listening to their advice about my marriage. The guilt was a heavy burden, but they never scolded. Lu'anna and I were both cherished until my appreciation knew no bounds.

I knew how much Dad had always looked forward to my wedding. That disastrous marriage just seemed a punishment for ignoring his dreams. I was filled with contempt for myself. Sowing the seeds of rebellion I had reaped sorrow – not only for myself, but also for my loved ones. It bothered me for years until I gave my life to Jesus and He taught me to forgive – myself as well as others.

It was six months before I braved living on my own again. Moving back to Providence, I sought work, but knew only how to keep house and cook. Jobs were scarce, but some house cleaning work was available. After a while, with some help from welfare, it was possible to get a little apartment for Lu'anna and me. Life wasn't easy, but Dad had always taught me to save "for a rainy day." I put everything possible aside for whatever might be around the next corner.

In 1959 it seemed wise to get away from all the heartache that filled my memories. Why do we think moving will solve every problem? More often that not, it adds new ones to those we take along! My destination was New York City. Lu'anna was three, so I decided to buy her clothes before going. Our savings of $375 seemed a lot, but with no job waiting, I sold everything except clothes and a few personal items, to have all the cash possible. That did indeed prove wise!

Off we went to a "better" life, where I knew only one person. He, who had been like a relative in the past, found us a room in the same hotel in which he lived. It was large with a bath, and it cost me twenty-nine dollars a week. It had no kitchen, so I used my friend's.

So many wrong decisions! Aware he and his roommate were homosexual, I saw no danger. Surely they would not be a problem to me. How could I have been so foolish? Not knowing the Lord, and unaware that His Word said they were sinning, it was both ignorant and blind for me to believe this. So much of the world is this way. Only Jesus and His Word can shed light where Satan and his darkness are in control.

New York City was, and is, every bit as evil as they say! All kinds of creeps are out to get anyone they can. Getting lost on the subways can be dangerous, and it is terrifying. It happened more than one time to me! As crime is everywhere, a person has to be constantly alert.

It was months before I found work at a laundry, and the money was almost gone. They didn't pay much, and the heat and humidity caused me to lose a lot of weight. While earning barely enough money for food and to meet Lu'anna's needs, I got sick and had to quit.

Pride saw welfare as a last resort and refused it. I shudder today, remembering what it was like to job hunt in that huge city. With subways to fight, pimps looking for desperate girls in need of work, and weirdos on the prowl, it was terrible!

Eventually a hospital hired me and that paid somewhat better, as there was overtime available. I enjoyed being a nurse's aid and loved taking care of sick people. When patients were really ill or dying, I prayed for them in my own way. Many improved and were able to go home.

One lady especially stays in my memory. An alcoholic, she took a liking to me. When being released, she asked if I would work for her on my days off. She was very good to me and paid me well. I wasn't saved at the time, but the Lord used my prayers. She got better and drank less, though later she moved away, and I don't know what happened after that.

As a child I always felt deep inside me that things would get better. Even in the Children's Center, it seemed as if I knew in my heart that my life had a special purpose. I had a compassion for children who had no parents, or who had only one parent. Also, I was drawn to the elderly, seeming to get wisdom from them. Especially if they weren't well, I loved old people. My grandmother's illness may explain why hospitals have always attracted me.

My friend at the hotel worked days, so he kept Lu'anna while I was on the graveyard shift. That seemed the only choice I had, as people in New York could not be trusted to babysit. Most were doing something illegal or were on drugs.

Being a nurses' aid at the hospital didn't pay that well, so I was often forced into overtime to make ends meet. It was hard, demanding work. As I usually came home exhausted, there wasn't much time to spend with my little girl. That is something I still regret. Her babysitter and his roommate suddenly began having overnight parties. They were involved with some very undesirable people, which made me afraid for Lu'anna. Thinking she might be molested, I was forced to make a change.

A live-in housekeeping job paid better, but that meant Lu'anna and I would be separated. A Christian couple was available to board her, but time together would only be on my days off. Considering the religious convictions of the couple, I was sure her care would improve. But oh the pain! It seemed the only way, but it tore my heart out.

Lu'anna was well fed and the care was excellent for only sixteen dollars a week. The new job meant I could save something for the future, but how I missed that child! She was all I had and night after night, that lonely mother cried herself to sleep.

Knowing that my child was suffering brought back painful memories of my own abandonment. As I hurt for her, depression struck again. A voice kept whispering, "You have failed as a mother and in every other way. Why not end your life?" At the time, I knew nothing about Satan. Now I know that the devil loves to torture anyone God plans to use to bring Him souls!

Sometimes I took alcohol to soothe me, but it only added to the depression. Eventually everything made me ill, and I got behind in paying Lu'anna's board. Once recovered, I went to see them. That "Christian" woman had decided she wanted my little daughter for her own. "You owe us a debt and cannot pay," she said, as if it were all settled, "so we keep the child!"

Horrified, I pleaded, "But I'll pay! Honest! Only you must let me do it a little at a time."

She refused, saying, "You haven't lived up to our bargain, so Lu'anna's mine. I have every right to keep her!"

Absolutely desperate, I went to the police. God moved and miracles began happening. Those tough, busy policemen had patience with that sobbing mother, as she cried, "My baby! My Lu'anna is being taken from me!" When they asked what I meant, it all came pouring out. That they were able to understand that distraught woman was a miracle in itself.

One big Irish cop exclaimed, "Why, that's meaner'n feeding cocaine to a dog!" Knowing he wanted me to smile, I tried but couldn't. He insisted, "Tell us where the witch lives so we can spike her guns!"

Difficult as it is to believe, they took me to see a judge whose court was actually in session. Not only were we allowed to interrupt, but he asked, "Did you sign anything which gives the child to them?"

Upon hearing that I definitely had not, he said, "You boys go and get that little girl. Go right away, they might leave and take her away." He looked at me with such compassion, saying, "You must sign a statement first, though, promising to pay the bill when possible."

It was truly an example of God's love, and of His grace. Alone and broke, I had no hope of getting Lu'anna back. His great loving hand reached down, in the midst of that uncaring city, to help us.

Oh the joy of being together again! Though illness had once more taken my savings, I was determined to keep her with me. We lived with friends for a while, sharing the rent. When I found a job, it was necessary again to take the graveyard shift so they could babysit. They lived a wild life and that worried me. Again, there seemed no alternative. Coming from work, I would find the house full of people who had been drinking all night. Their loud music made sleep impossible.

I would come home exhausted, needing rest, but time with Lu'anna was imperative. As the only child in the building, she was lonely. To escape from that hectic situation, we saw most of the movies in town. At that time Central Park was peaceful and quiet, as it isn't now. We enjoyed it, just being together. It was wonderful to get away from all that racket where we lived.

The situation soon became too much for me to handle was neither the environment I wanted for Lu'anne, nor the people for her to be around. Looking back, welfare would seem the logical answer, but again pride made the decision. To me it always seemed important for her to have what other children had. As welfare wasn't much in those days, overtime paid better. Only it stole from our being together. Always there seemed a lack of time and of money!

Finally I decided to put Lu'anna in a temporary foster home with Helen Johnson. Totally unaware of it, I began to walk in Dad's footsteps, as far as my child was concerned. Mrs. Johnson lived in New Jersey and had children of her own. Fifteen dollars a week didn't sound bad and she appeared to be a good person. I was impressed by the clean house and knew Lu'anna needed the companionship of other people. We could spend my days off together and it would get her away from that troubling environment.

One day something said to pay them an unexpected visit. Mrs. Johnson was no more surprised than was I. What a shock! Both the house and Lu'anna were filthy. My daughter's hair had not been combed for days. The tangles were almost impossible to get out. Again that lost woman I used to be without Jesus found herself in turmoil!

Moving my child was the only choice, but it meant our savings would once again dwindle. I have always been grateful for Dad's advice about saving for "rainy days."

Being off work to look for another sitter meant no income at all. Today women in that situation have help and I thank God for it. There were no day care centers then. Any mother alone had to find a solution for herself.

Personally, I believe mothers should not leave home to work if it is at all possible for them to stay at home. Especially while their children are small. They need them close, but circumstances force people to do what they may look back on with regret later. Yet, at the time, they are doing the only thing that they can do.

Of all people, I understand the tremendous pressures. Today it is very plain to see that my own priorities were not in order during those years. Not knowing Jesus, I had no plan for my life. Without the bible there was no handbook, and without Him, no director. How fortunate are those young mothers who have both!

I was deeply depressed and didn't know where to turn. Pride is expensive and often robs us. It kept me from going home to Cape Cod. I didn't want Dad to know about our difficulties, as the family might think of me as a failure. Independence can be either a virtue or a flaw in one's character, depending on its source. Prideful independence cost Lu'anna my companionship and robbed me of hers.

Wading deep in depression and turmoil, I deserve no credit that adoption was never even contemplated. Neither did I think of foster homes on a permanent basis. The Lord was in control though I didn't know Jesus personally then, or realize that He cared. Lu'Anna had always seemed a gift to me from God and no matter what, she was mine! In God's Word, Proverbs 16:18 KJV tells us, "Pride goeth before destruction, and a haughty spirit before a fall." I seemed to walk very near destruction and took my share of falls!

Why is pride a sin in God's eyes? A prideful person cannot be blessed, for he puts himself ahead of God. From that untenable position, he must fall! It breaks the first commandment ikn Exodus 20:3, "thou shalt have no other gods before me." In Jeremiah 13:17, God says He weeps secretly for our pride.

Once we step into the position, "I can do it better myself," we sin. Like a small child determined to cross the busy street alone, there is danger ahead! The Lord Jesus Christ wants us to reach for His help. He wants us to expect it to be waiting. He reaches down, yet too often pride slaps away that loving Hand.

Who is pride's master? It is the soul's enemy, Satan. I know now that god's mercy kept me going. Only He knew I would one day be His disciple. Through ignorance due to lack of religious teaching, the devil had me bound through pride and self will. He tried to keep it that way, but God's power is greater. Nothing could stop the divine plan for my life. Praise the Name of Jesus.

4

Joe, Jobs, and Jesus

It seemed I had been unhappy forever. Then Joe Brown came along, bringing laughter and happiness. What a great personality that man had! With him around, a person felt good, even if life seemed bleak.

While striving not to board Lu'anna in another home, I was open to almost any solution. Lonely and worn out, I felt a failure. Nothing had turned out as expected. Joe brought me a new life. It was thrilling just to be around him. To a desperate woman, he seemed the only way out.

No Robert Redford in appearance, yet he seemed kind and appeared to care for Lu'anna. Lonely for his own daughter, he was quite attentive to mine. Again I saw what I wanted to see, not the man as he really was.

I knew Joe was divorced and hurting. Like me, he was trying to fill the emptiness in his own life. He worked at a restaurant as a short order cook, and made pretty good money. I knew that, but little else about Joe Brown. Before long I knew too much. Some of his appeal was the promise that I could stay home with my little girl. I so longed to do that, immorality didn't seem too high a price to pay. Tired of battling on my own, I was discouraged. I wanted a more normal life and longed for time with Lu'anna.

Joe and I decided to live together, so we moved into an apartment over the restaurant. It was cheap as well as convenient for him. Love didn't enter into it for either of us. We were two lonely, wounded people searching for someone who cared. We shared nothing but failed marriages. That brought some understanding of one another's needs, but little else.

Searching for happiness can lead down dangerous paths. I soon found Joe's lifestyle was not what I had expected. Night after night we were at the neighborhood bar. Everybody knew the owners were racketeers. I wasn't aware, however, that they were also selling drugs. Nor did I know that Joe was hooked on drugs! Again, that peace for which I had longed lay shattered at my feet.

So easily I could have become an addict in that atmosphere, but God kept me safe. Often since then I have thanked Him for protection which was not even recognized at the time. It was a fast life. We drank until the place closed down at four a.m., then slept all day until Joe went to work at two in the afternoon. Of course, I wasn't spending time with Lu'anna as I had planned. Not wanting her exposed to that kind of life, I sought help from Joe's Aunt Lucille. She lived in Brooklyn and agreed to care for my daughter. As we lived in Manhattan, that meant another hated separation.

Eventually we did move to Brooklyn with Joe commuting to work. When I found a job at the hospital, his aunt kept Lu'anna. It was only a half a block between our houses, and that was much better. I was searching for something illusive, a deeper satisfaction with life. I wasn't happy, not with myself, my work, nor with Joe. There can be no peace for one living without Christ. At times contentment seemed almost within my grasp. Yet it always escaped, leaving me miserable again.

There are only two choices of master, God or Satan. Over and over the Word tells us that. When we opt to serve the Devil, he makes sure our minds are tormented with insecurity and harassed with anxiety. Oh, he gives a false peace to those who know nothing about God. But anyone knowing the Lord exists yearns for something more. There is an empty hole that nothing can fill. Nothing but Jesus Christ.

People try to fill it with material possessions, but they fail. Others try drugs, alcohol, or sex – but nothing works. Why? Because when Jesus enters a heart He brings love. Man's soul yearns for that Love. God created us in His image, to give love. The human kind never measures up. His love is unselfish, compassionate and bottomless. It is perfectly described in God's Word. I Corinthians 13.

Satan always tortures that one that God sees as His own. The Devil is determined that we not accept Jesus as Lord. That spells his own defeat. His job is to "kill, steal, and destroy," but Jesus Christ comes "to give us life more abundantly." John 10:10.

Satan wins a victory whenever a person rejects Christ. Likewise, he knows anybody finding Him as Saviour will recognize the enemy. Satan is a liar and thief, who doesn't fight fair. He has no scruples. Winning is the only game in town as far as he is concerned.

Needing more room so Lu'anna could live with us, Joe and I moved into a larger place. They seemed to get along well, and he tried to be a good father. Joe Brown was an easy person to live with, except when he was drinking. Alcohol had its hold on the man. Whenever that demon was in control he grew nasty. I drank, too, but could handle nothing stronger than beer. Of course, you can get drunk on enough beer!

Happiness was always snatched from my hands, but I didn't know why. Part of the time Joe and I were content with one another and our lives. At others, both of us were miserable. I was no angel, and could stir up conflicts for no reason. As Lu'Anna came to love him, however, I grew fonder of Joe.

He treated me like royalty during the pregnancy. It was a really happy time. While joyfully anticipating another child, we three did become more a family. Lu'anna had spent most of her seven years alone. I was aware of that, and understood her loneliness. Yet we had to be careful about her playmates. The neighborhood youngsters were a rough bunch.

New York is a difficult place in which to rear children. During the sixties drugs were getting easier to find and more people had accepted that lifestyle. Children were exposed to them when they were five or six years old. Again, God was good – He kept Lu'anna and later her two sisters, from the drug culture. He is merciful, even when people reject or ignore Him.

When Joann was born I expected things to be different. Again, disappointment stole our happiness. That sorrow-free life I thought others lived wasn't to be mine. Satan never wanted me to find that peace for which I yearned. Usually he attacks our minds. Often it is through our children. As Joe and I were preparing to take little Joann home, the doctor came in.

"You can't take her today," he said.

"We're all ready to go!" I exclaimed, "why not?" As he looked sadly toward our baby, fear swooped down upon me.

"Because of a heart defect," the doctor said. "We must keep a close watch on her for a few days, and take some tests!"

It seemed like hell broke loose in that hospital room! How terrible to realize that our newborn child, who looked perfect in every way, had a heart condition. Tears flowing, I asked, "How could that happen? My family never had any heart trouble."

Turning angrily to Joe, I accused, "this has to be your fault!" It seemed I had to lash out at somebody. The doctor tried to calm me, but it took quite a while.

The hardest thing yet was walking out of that building without little Joann. Of course, it was equally difficult for Joe. For all his faults, that man never missed a day visiting her. In less than a week, we took her home. Frightened, I was overly protective.

The hardest thing yet was walking out of that building without little Joann. Of course, it was equally difficult for Joe. For all his faults, that man never missed a day visiting her. In less than a week, we took her home. Frightened, I was overly protective.

Joann had to be taken to the clinic every two weeks for the next three months. It was then changed to once a month until she was four years old. The doctors had explained about the hole in her heart, but it never caused any discomfort. She appeared normal, was always hungry, and ate well. None of the usual symptoms ever surfaced, but I worried terribly.

Satan knows exactly where to attack each of us! Unhappy with Joe, I was disappointed with our life and really anxious about Joan. Satan wanted me miserable. His goal was suicide and he nearly succeeded. God's plan for my life would then have been aborted. The devil is an expert at using the precise thing which will drive one to the edge.

The child I had so anticipated he used against me. Somehow her illness opened wounds in me dating back to the Children's Center. Wounds from that first marriage, too, were reopened. Depression returned. It is one of Satan's best allies, and together they make a formidable pair. Praise God, the Devil didn't win! Somebody was praying – somewhere.

We saw a miracle. Joann was four when I took her to a meeting at the Automox Ballroom where a man of God was ministering. His gift was the discerning of spirits. He prayed for Joann, then exclaimed, "God shows me this child has a hole in her heart!" I was amazed, but I knew it had to be the Lord. He continued, "She must be anointed with oil for seven days and seven nights, then God will heal her."

I did exactly as he said to do. Later, when the doctors X-rayed Joann, they were astonished, for no operation was necessary. Surgery had always loomed like a black cloud over her head. God takes care of His own, and she was destined to be His. Praise His Name! Joann is still the healthiest of my three girls.

Always seeking jobs that paid well, I later found one as a barmaid at a tavern. Totally unaware that the Mafia owned it, I asked another girl working with me, "Why do those men kiss each other on the cheek?"

"Because they're gonna knock somebody off," she replied.

"Knock somebody off? What's that?" Impossible to explain, living where we did, but I was naive.

"Boy, are you dumb!" she said with disgust, "kill somebody, that's what it means!"

Occasionally some regular would disappear, as if walking off a cliff. We girls appreciated the tight way it was run, so we asked no questions. In such a dangerous area, that made us feel safe. The owners were involved in the numbers racket and finally sucked me into that form of gambling. Somehow it never seemed evil, but more like playing Bingo. You could win a lot of money.

I stand in awe now at how the Lord protected me physically from the wickedness in New York. Even working for the Mafia, I was treated well. We were really in Satan's playground. Leaving the organization usually means a death sentence, but I made it out. Working there must have exposed me to many dangers, but God was faithful!

Becky joined her sisters when they were three and ten. She was a really good baby and healthy. Joe had always wanted a boy, having fathered three girls, including one that was not mine. This was disappointing to him. I believe the seeds of rejection in Becky's life were planted right then. *He* couldn't help feeling this way. Parents usually aren't aware of the problem, but a baby senses it. Feelings do not have to be voiced to affect a child.

My advice to expectant mothers and fathers is always, "Don't expect or plan on either sex. Pray that the baby is healthy and let God make the decision. That way no harm will come to the child."

A year or so later, my barmaid career blossomed into a really good job for the summer. A black man and wife owned a fancy lodge at Perth Amboy, New Jersey. Having watched me at the tavern, they appreciated my speed at bartending. From the owners there they knew I was honest and trustworthy. Wealthy people came to their place to dance, eat, and drink. Whether illegal activities, such as gambling, went on I couldn't say. It certainly drew the right clientele and lots of money.

After working there quite a while, I was serving drinks one night and got really dizzy. The room seemed to spin, though I hadn't been drinking. For weeks depression had ridden me until tears flowed for no reason. That night my boss, who was kind and always concerned about us, insisted I go upstairs to lie down. He sent his wife along to help. She got me settled in one of the beds, switched off the light and left.

Hoping to sleep away whatever was wrong, I cuddled under the covers. With no warning, light filled the room brighter than it was before she left. I got up to investigate, and the switch was turned off. It obviously wasn't a hallucination, for the room was bright as day. Unable to figure out what was going on, I stood there. Then realized, with astonishment, that the illness had suddenly and totally, disappeared.

Abruptly a thought entered my head, as if someone spoke, "You aren't to return to this place."

Puzzling about it all, I went back to work. Though the job paid well, I felt it necessary to give notice immediately.

"If it's more money you want," the boss coaxed, "we'll raise your wages."

I really wanted to explain, but didn't understand myself what was happening. "No, it isn't that," I had to keep saying. "I just won't be back anymore." The Lord was leading me though I knew almost nothing about Him. There was no possible doubt! That voice in my head must be obeyed, but I couldn't figure out why. Or from whence it came!

I really wanted to explain, but didn't understand myself what was happening. "No, it isn't that," I had to keep saying. "I just won't be back anymore." The Lord was leading me though I knew almost nothing about Him. There was no possible doubt! That voice in my head must be obeyed, but I couldn't figure out why. Or from whence it came!

Many people can look back on such times. God loves us enough to get our attention. He may put you in jail, allow Satan to steal your health, or switch on a light – whatever it takes.

He watched His own Son hang on that cross, without sending "legions of angels" to help. Why? Because His love is the greatest force in the universe. It knows no bounds. God's love walks into a bar. There is no place He won't enter – and has – to find his chosen ones. Jesus died that the world might be saved. The Word of God says so in John 3:16! Praise His Name.

One day in September, 1968, when Becky was 16 months old, Aunt Lucille was supposed to go with me to a meeting. In Manhattan, a so-called minister was in the "numbers" racket, which pertained to horse racing. The report was that he gave out only wining numbers. That sounded exciting. By then I was heavily involved in gambling, which is almost as addictive as drugs. The numbers racket, like any other kind of gambling, ruins lives, steals from families, and pulls victims into other evils.

After waiting for some time, I sent Lu'anna the half block to ask Aunt Lucille when we were going. My daughter returned to say, "Auntie can't go to Manhattan."

I asked, "Well, why not? She wanted to yesterday!"

"Because of a book. It's so interesting she can't stop."

"Good Lord!" I exclaimed with disgust, "What kind of book?"

"Something about religion. She says it's wonderful!"

Never long on patience, I was getting upset. "That minister has sure-fire winning numbers," I told Lu'anna, "but I'm not going down there by myself."

"Well, Auntey don't plan to leave that book," Lu'anna said with a grin. "She wouldn't hardly talk to me!"

"There are so many different religions in New York." I said, "no telling what she's mixed up in." After thinking a moment, I added, "Go back and tell her I want to read that book when she's done."

Though aggravated about missing the chance to gamble, I was interested in spite of myself. That book might be about Jehovah Witnesses. THey often came to our door. Aunt Lucille might need some straightening out.

It took quite a while, but she finally sent the book over and it was sure enough interesting! Titled *God Is the Answer,* it turned my life topsy turvy. The introduction was especially intriguing, "God said He would save, heal, and deliver readers as they turn these pages." I needed some excitement, but that sounded pretty weird.

Once into that book, I couldn't put it down either! Reading it straight through before going to sleep, I knew some changes sounded pretty weird.

Once into that book, I couldn't put it down either! Reading it straight through before going to sleep, I knew some changes had come over me. It seemed God had actually spoken through those pages, and I felt clean. Clean and changed, for the "ministers" with the lucky numbers held no fascination at all, or did he ever again, praise the Lord!

God Is the Answewr had touched me so deeply I wanted to meet the author, Geraldine McDaniel. She was an Evangelist at Trinity Holy Church. When I decided to go there and check things out, she was playing the piano. Of course, I didn't know it then. When the invitation was given to come to the altar it meant nothing to me. Then, someone asked if I was saved.

My ignorant, "No, I'm Catholic," must have sounded funny, but nobody laughed.

Another person explained, "We aren't asking about your religion, but whether you know Jesus as personal Saviour?"

I said, "Yes." Surely everybody knew Jesus was the Baby in a manger at Christmas. Those people explained, lovingly, what "Saviour" meant, but I didn't go forward. Nobody was going to do that "laying on of hands" business to me! Not so you'd notice it! Before leaving, though I explained about reading the book and they suggested I return.

The following week Aunt Lucille and I went back. We were really blessed by the service, so we kept returning. Unaware of hunger, I was being fed! In October I went forward for the altar call and was saved.

Probably I was started down that path as a child, when Dad's Uncle Albert prayed for my salvation. I believe his prayers were used to lead me to Jesus, though it took years. Fortunately, he lived to be ninety! Always independent, I had seen no need for a Saviour in my life! That proves the importance of praying for unsaved loved ones! It should be a deep commitment, for God is faithful! He truly will save "our house." Acts 16:34!

Aunty also found her Saviour at Trinity Church. I tried to explain our new experiences to Joe, but he wanted no part of salvation. A lifestyle in the "fast lane" suited him fine. In his eyes, Aunty and I had moved over to the slow one. Unable to handle all that "religion," Joe checked out of my life for keeps.

From time to time, the girls hear from him, but he never could see that God is the Answer.

The Bible says our sins are washed away in the Blood of Christ. Forgiveness is part of the package – for everybody. Because he died for all my sins, I walk free today. In Psalm 86:5 we learn that the Lord is always ready to forgive and "plenteous in mercy" unto all them that call upon Him. (KJV)

After asking God for that gift of forgiveness – which is available only because of His grace – I then had to forgive myself. That meant remembering, crying, and praying. It took a while!

Only then could I go back home to say, "Mom and Dad, Jesus is now my Saviour. Having received His forgiveness, I ask yours." Tears in their eyes forced me to admit, "I soon learned you were right about that seaman." After we hugged, this "sheep that had been found," said, "You were so loving when Lu'anna and I came home. Nobody ever scolded about that awful mistake." By then tears were flowing all around. "There aren't enough words to say 'thank you.' "

Dad insisted, "You don't have to thank anybody, Shirley. We were glad to have you and that baby home and safe!"

Having accepted Jesus as Saviour and been obedient about asking forgiveness, I felt new in body and mind. It was easy to understand what Paul meant in II Corinthians 5:17. "A new creature in Christ." Truly, old things had passed away!

The following January I was reading God's Word at home. Suddenly, while praising Him, I began to speak in a new language. It didn't frighten me, as others had talked about the Baptism in the Holy Spirit. In fact, a new joy seemed to fill my heart and soul. When younger I had often teased the Chinese people about their language. Plainly that was what came pouring from my lips. God must have chosen it as my first prayer language to humble me! Or because He has a sense of humor. I joined Trinity Holy Church and was active there for three years, doing everything from cleaning the church to singing in the choir. Their missionary work consisted of passing out tracts on the streets and visiting hospitals, so I did that, too. We saw lots of fruit – changed lives – among those street people. When they accompanied us to church. Evangelist McDaniel's welcome was sincere. You couldn't find anybody too dirty for her to love.

I was ordained at Trinity, where God called me to be an Evangelist. A while earlier my mother in the Lord, Evangelist McDaniels, had prophecied that would soon happen. I shall always be indebted to that precious saint of God.

The introduction to her book was certainly prophetic, for I got saved and delivered from Satan's bondage through it. As did many others! She still has a ministry of healing and deliverance at Trinity, at 199 St. James St., Brookly. Now I love that servant of God, and I thank Him for her!

5

God Proves Faithful

When the Lord said I was to minister in Sing Sing, my reaction was near disbelief. "How am I to do that, Father?"

His reply came immediately, "Go and ask the Chaplain's permission to minister." I had found by then if God was in something it worked. That is, if I was obedient.

Though my knees were nervous, they took me on some trips! One bus, four subways, and a taxi later, I arrived at the huge place. A grey maximum security facility in New York State, it was forboding to say the least. When God asks us to do something, if we are obedient and wait patiently upon *His* timing, gates will open. Even gates at a maximum security prison!

Of course, the Chaplain said, "Yes, I always need help."

My ministry was blessed there, as inmates found Jesus as their Lord and Saviour. God healed and delivered, as His Word promises. Knowing little about such things, I learned He knew a lot!

Robert, a dear friend's son, and another fellow robbed a gas station. The other man shot an attendant, then blamed it on Robert. He was incarcerated for the crime, and expected to spend many years in Sing Sing. It was a thrill beyond description to have my friend's son kneel and receive Jesus as Saviour. That is something which never grows old – leading someone to give his or her heart to Jesus Christ. Robert began reading his Bible and soon afterward, was filled with the Holy Spirit.

Next, he began to preach to Gospel to the other inmates. While praying for him, as I did often for my new converts, I had a vision. He was in a truck being taken away from Sing Sing. It seemed I ran to catch up and say, "You will be getting out sooner than you think!"

When I shared it with Robert, he felt that was impossible. Though he loved the Lord, he could see no way his sentence might be changed so quickly? He was excited, nevertheless, and began believing for it to happen.

His mother and I fasted and prayed, also believing God for his release. Not much later it was beautiful to hear that Robert would be out ahead of schedule, just as I had seen! He is not preaching outside of prison walls.

Soon afterward, the girls and I moved from Brooklyn to Laurelton, Queens, but still in New York City. The Lord said I was to hold prayer meetings at home. He brought kids there to be saved and filled with the Holy Spirit. Many were delivered from rebellion, drug addiction, and other things when I laid hands on them. He was using that Shirley who earlier was determined nobody would ever lay hands on her! God's ways are certainly not the ways of man. Romans 11:33.

Soon my girls were saved and baptized in the Spirit also. God used them in mighty ways! At nine Joann was giving prophetic messages to churches – about what they were to do. She was also used that way to edify and to heal. Much of what God said through her is being fulfilled today. She was called to preach the Gospel at an early age.

Lu'anna was being used in prophecy also – mostly to individuals, and it was definitely of God. She often prayed for the sick, and God healed them.

An evangelist asked us to pray for his mother who wouldn't go to church. He was filled with the Holy Ghost, in fact, a deliverance minister. We arrived at the lady's home to find her mentally disturbed – her conversation made no sense at all.

Offering to pray for her, I had just begun when Lu'anna got up. The Holy Spirit had said for her to lay hands on that woman and cast out the demon. I was still awaiting directions from the Lord when Lu'anna began to minister. The demon left, screaming. After lying on the floor a half hour, that lady got up, praising the Lord. From that day on she talked normally. My daughter, only seventeen, was truly being used of God. I was both amazed and delighted.

All three of the girls prayed and praised God as they saw Him move. It was prophecied that Becky would be used musically, but that hasn't come to pass yet.

We adults always covered the children at those times with God's Word and with His Blood. Demons delight to enter into innocent children, and will if they are not protected.

In the early 70's New York City was a dangerous place to be. The gangs were really bad. Teenagers, armed with baseball bats, knives, and even guns took their war games seriously. The 'Immortals" was a Spanish gang and tough. Members of another gang, the "Black Spades" were proud of their color and heritage. War constantly raged between them, and with others. Any excuse would inflame them, but race never failed. Their code demanded that if a member was injured by another group, his gang had to get revenge.

They were vicious, and not only to other gangs. Old people were often beaten, and their purses or wallets snatched. One of the weird "sports" was breaking into houses to rob or burn them. Younger kids were always fair game. Gang members beat them and took their money. Yet the Lord gave me a love and a burden for these rough teenagers. He let me to witness to many of them.

Any given day, ten to twenty boys might be in and out of our house. My daughters and I prayed with them and I saw a number receive Christ and get filled with the Holy Ghost. It was exciting to have those new converts go out then and witness about Christ to other kids.

We fed them physical food as well as spiritual. The police in that neighborhood were overwhelmed because violence diminished daily. "We have to give you credit for what is going on," more than one said to me. "You are doing wonders with these kids and we couldn't change them at all!" Of course, that opened another door as I explained it was the Lord, not I, turning those lives around.

As I moved about the country, it became impossible for me to keep up with all of those youngsters. However, the Lord blessed me three years ago during a visit to New York City. One of my sons in the Lord, Harry Gonzales, arranged for meetings with several of them. What a joy that was!

Tyrone Johnson had been in one of the gangs. He was saved during that period and filled with the Holy Spirit. How I praise God that he is now preaching the Gospel, praying for the sick, and also into prophecy. He found his calling as an Evangelist right there in Laurelton. Tyrone's mother was a Christian who kept her children in prayer over the years. Again, the Lord did His part!

Terry O'Neal, my daughter in the Lord, had planned to become a Muslim. Saved at our home, Terry received the Holy Spirit, with His gifts in evidence. She is still using what God gave her that day. How grateful I am for the Lord's using me as an instrument in those young lives. Geraldine McDaniel's book totally changed not only my life, but theirs as well.

I pray often for them and know the Lord is ever watchful to care for His own. There is absolutely no distance in prayer. Though I don't know exactly where each one is, God does. His arm is long enough to do whatever may be necessary.

Those children were "on the streets" because nobody cared where most of them were or what they did. Love was a stranger in many of the homes, where parents were too busy to cherish them. Busy doing what? Partying, doing drugs, most simply didn't care what happened to their children. Too often the parents had grown up in that same environment, where close loving families were a rarity. The same conditions exist today, but have spread across the nation.

Those children were searching for attention, and preferred being in trouble to being ignored. (Of course, that isn't unique to those in poverty. Children of affluent parents often get into trouble for the same reason.)

Some of the violence was due to hunger. The really deprived children felt driven to rob and kill to survive. Sometimes they had smaller brothers or sisters at home, crying for food. My girls and I didn't have much, but we shared with those less fortunate, and God took care of us.

The Lord instilled in my heart not only a love for those young people, but He showed me the need to fast one day a week for them. Some think we fight a physical battle, but that is wrong. We are in a spiritual war. II Corinthians 10:4 tells us that our warfare is not of flesh and blood but "mighty before God for the destruction of strongholds."

It is past time for us to wake up and stand up. We must look to Jesus who is our strength and our deliverer. The battle is not ours, but His. Psalm 24:8 tells us where our strength lies, "The Lord is strong and mighty."

Once we have joined God's army, we are overcomers, but it works only if we lean totally on Him. I have seen it happen, over and over again, Jesus is victor whenever the devil loses a slave. As one reaches out to the Light that is Jesus Christ, he realizes the darkness is Satan's. Our Lord is in the business of changing lives!

One of those young men is now called "Reverend Wilson." He was pushing drugs when he was shot. To this day he insists, "Satan did it," and has never named a person. He was found on the street, dying. When his sister heard he was hospitalized and in a coma, she asked for help. At his bedside we prayed, "Raise him up to be a minister, Lord, and give him favor with the judge."

God answered that prayer and has also filled him with the Holy Ghost. He decided to hold a street revival shortly after being released. His sister and I helped, plus members of another church. Getting permission from the police, we roped off an area in a bad part of New York City. Lesbians, drug pushers, addicts, pimps – all thought it was their "turf."

The meeting started early in the morning and lasted until midnight. Because it was Satan's territory, the young people formed a circle to keep him out. Reverend Wilson preached as if he couldn't stop. It was exciting to see those wallowing in such sin come forward to be saved. Many of the lesbians' partners tried to break through that circle of believers. They wanted to get their girlfriends out. We pled the blood of Jesus and they were powerless before It.

That meeting lasted two days. Reverend Wilson continued in the ministry – watching souls get away from Satan. At last report, he was in the South, ministering to his own father, among others.

Next, He led me into hospitals. At St. Mary's in New York city many people were saved. Sister Mary Sherman had a ministry at Queen's General Hospital, and we became close friends. Every Sunday we held services there. She also had a Friday prayer meeting at home. What an inspiration that lady was to me while I raised three girls alone. She now pastors a church.

A book, *God Is the Answer,* was used to save me. More importantly God's own Word has kept me that way. It not only teaches how to live so we please Him, but John 1:1 says God and His Word are one! Verse 14 tells us the Word became flesh and "dwelt among us."

People ask sometimes, "Weren't you scared during those years you were ministering in New York?"

I have to reply, "When any situation was threatening, God always intervened."

Others have asked, "New York gangs are so dangerous. Where did you find courage to minister to them?"

"It was God," is my only answer. "He put such love in me for those lost children, there was no room for anything else." That is absolutely true. I ached to help them find the Lord, for nobody ever needed His love and peace more. I have sometimes tried to explain those years by saying, "There wasn't time to be afraid. God was moving and I had to run just to keep up!"

It is difficult to explain God's protection to those who don't know Jesus as Saviour. Like His peace, it just is! He never promised his soldiers that they would have a smooth road. Yet those two – His peace and His protection – ever march beside us.

Spiritually speaking, there are two armies, God's and Satan's. The Bible explains why that is. Which to choose is a personal decision, and upon it hangs our place in eternity. Jesus Christ is the only door through which one can enter God's army. John 10:9 says, "If any man enter in he shall be saved."

His recruits will have their hearts and minds guarded. Philippians 4:7. There is no need to fear ever again, which makes that army unlike all others. Even the Pentagon cannot promise what God does.

Satan ever keeps his soldiers in turmoil. They find no peace. One is protected only at the whim of his general. Worry and frustration march beside Hell's soldiers, for without Jesus there is no real peace.

In the Amplified Bible, Philippians 4:7 tells us that God's peace is "that tranquil state of a soul assured of its salvation through Christ, and so fearing nothing from God and content with its earthly lot ... that peace, which transcends all understanding, SHALL GARRISON AND MOUNT GUARD over your hearts and minds in Christ Jesus."

Is it any wonder Satan's people find that difficult to comprehend? Once we are "assured" of our soul's salvation, everything else falls into place. No wonder we are called a "peculiar people," who shout "hallelujah" and mean it!

The word "assured" is code. When a person invites Jesus into his heart, yet feels no semblance of repentance, he wanders about seeking that Peace. According to the Amplified Bible, John the Baptist shouted, "Repent – that is, think differently; change your mind, regretting your sins and changing your conduct – for the kingdom of heaven is at hand."

When there is no "change of conduct," Jesus has not been put on the throne as Lord. Of course, His peace cannot "garrison and mount guard" over a heart that is not truly His. That heart, instead of peace, holds fear! The word "assured" indicates Jesus has been enthroned and self demoted.

Oh, it is possible for even a Spirit-filled Christian to lose that peace. Looking at circumstances and problems, instead of at Jesus, can help Satan steal it. Instead of trusting their Lord, people take what Satan offers. He delights in convincing a Christian there *is* no hope. God never said the "way" would be problem-free. His promise is that if we keep our eyes on Him, those problems will be surmounted.

How does a child of God get in the position where there's no peace? Usually by entertaining Satan's thoughts, which are always negative. The Holy Ghosts offers only positive thoughts, and it is our job to "think on" His kind of thought, not the enemy's. Philippians 4:8. It is we who must "fix our mind" on things which are pure.

I have prayed for many – from young to elderly. God has touched those sick, afflicted or demon possessed in response to my prayers. Some, who said they had little faith, received miracles. Without my own faith, God might not have moved. Looking back, it boggles my mind. So many healed – from cancer, diabetes, and heart conditions. Eyes have been healed and vision returned. Depression has been chased away, for nothing is impossible with God.

The angel who told Mary she would bear God's son said, "For with God nothing is ever impossible, and no word from God shall be without power or impossible to fulfullment." Luke 1:37, Amp.

There is nothing beyond His power, if we but trust and believe. Christians seem to trust their doctors more than God. Those in the medical profession can fail, but He never does.

One of the greatest blessings for me happened, of all places, at O'Rourke's Children Center in Providence. God led me there soon after we moved. He knew those horrendous memories would help me to relate to the children in like situations. I was used as a "Cottage Mother."

Most of the boys under my care had been in gangs, drugs, and crime. When they began to pray for one another, and to read their Bibles, the Supervisor grew alarmed. He saw a great change in their behaviour and could not understand it.

My boys were some of the worst at the Center, yet the Lord changed many of them. I prayed with them individually, though it was risky. Prayer or counseling was forbidden cottage mothers. Several of the boys requested weekend passes to accompany me to church.

I was astonished when the authorities granted that first pass! God worked miracles, not only in young lives, but also in the system!

Each morning before going to work, I prayed that God become real in every young life. Many hours were spent in intercessory prayer and in fasting. Those two are mighty weapons, and cannot be emphasized enough. God works miracles through them, if we but do our part. Jesus fasted and prayed many hours – sometimes all night. Such dedication is rare in the church world today.

I have seen those two spiritual weapons – fasting and intercessory prayer – break the yoke of bondage so many times! Then the captive goes free. Unfortunately too many churches teach today that "they were for olden times." Why don't they realize Jesus left His power with us?

God's Word, in Matthew 23:18 and Mark 16:16 makes that very clear! If we disobey and refuse to fast and pray. He cannot bless us. Nor can He touch those for whom we are burdened. Satan tells God's people, "You can't fast, it might make you sick." They believe it, though Jesus said in the Word that the devil was a liar. John 8:44. Why does God's army believe anything Satan whispers? That seems to come easier than believing God!

Jesus said His people *would* fast – not might fast – after He was gone. It has always seemed like a commandment to me. Miracles so often happen during or after a fast consecrated to God, that I yearn to do it even more!

Do you wonder why fasting is important? Because Jesus did and He is our pattern, it is difficult to explain, but fasting cleanses us so that the Holy Spirit can flow through to do God's will. Not eating helps put down the fleshly or carnal side of our natures. Then the spiritual can rise to become dominant. Remember, Jesus fasted forty days and whipped Satan three times running. That's good enough for me! Matthew 4:1-11.

While I ministered in New York City, a friend's brother was shot pushing drugs. His sister and I went on a three day fast. We prayed, and he received Christ as Saviour. The Lord healed her brother, delivered him from drugs, and totally changed that young man. He decided to give himself up and received a sentence of ninety-nine years. That was what man thought. God had other plans.

Expecting to be jailed all his life, the boy began preaching Jesus Christ while in prison. Praise God, he was released about a year later. Fasting together – with prayer –

changes things! We were all delighted when he was given only a short probation. Now he is a minister, working for the Lord. How mighty is our God!

There were times when I found sums of money lying on the sidewalk in New York City. The Lord seemed to be saying, "You will never go hungry." Though a new Christian, I realized He was the source of all. Oh, but the Lord has been good to me! I love Him so much, and long ago I made a vow to serve Him until I die. That feeling has not changed, no matter what people say to me, or how they treat me.

Being a woman evangelist is not easy. Some men do not believe in females ministering, and lots of women don't believe in it either. Consequently, there is little support, either through prayer or financially. One must walk by faith, and faith alone. Hebrews 11:1-3.

When the girls and I moved to New Haven, Connecticut, Lu'anna was thinking about going into the Navy. Without funds for college, that seemed a way to get a good education., In less than six months, I was led to Christ's Chapel. There I worked with young people. God touched many lives and changed them.

I got sick shortly before Lu'anna left for the Navy. We had moved back to Providence, Rhode Island, where work was available in a hospital. Doctors there diagnosed a heart condition, and insisted that I stop working. I prayed and knew without doubt that God would heal me. After X-rays and many tests the physicians decided open heart surgery was necessary.

In the hospital that night, with an angiogram scheduled for the next morning, I prayed and prayed. The Lord showed me I had to ask forgiveness, because there was an 'aught' in my heart against somebody.

Matthew 5:23, KJV: "therefore if thou bring thy gift to the altar, and there rememberest that thy brother hath aught against thee; leave there thy gift before the altar, and go thy way; first be reconciled to thy brother, and then come and offer thy gift."

I truly thought I had forgiven Joe Brown, but the Lord said not. I prayed, "Father, I forgive the younger girls' father. I want to be totally cleansed of unforgiveness toward him." Immediately a supernatural healing came.

The next day, while preparing me for the angiogram, which can be a miserable experience, the doctors could find nothing wrong with my heart. Thank You, Jesus!

I had been unaware of the seriousness of my condition. As the cardiologist explained, I listened with amazement, "A valve was fast closing in your heart, and it has been healed." I praised God that the doctor could believe in miracles.

Lu'anna's being in the Navy was also God's providence. She sent much appreciated funds so that I could rest for a year. That money paid the rent and bought things for her sisters. While serving her country, she also received that education – as a laboratory technician. She has an excellent position in that field today.

Some years later doctors said that I had a thyroid problem. They also recommended radiation treatments, but I refused these, after only one treatment. After praying, There have been no more attacks, praise the Lord!

Knowing God can heal is half the battle. We must walk in faith and never in doubt! Satan's first order of business is planting doubt in our minds. Often he does it through loved ones who fear the consequences of our walking by faith. They see – with physical eyes – that we are ill. It is hard for them to understand why we, who see with spiritual eyes, insist God is healing us. Both of those times I *knew* God would heal me, absolutely knew it! Again, a year of rest and medication, while serving Him, made me totally well.

". . . and He cured all of them." Matthew 12:15 – Our Lord never said to anyone, "I'm sorry, but it isn't God's will for you to be healed." Time after time the Bible speaks of multitudes coming to Him and all were healed! Psalm 103:3 Amp – "Who forgives [every one of] all your iniquities, Who heals [each of] your diseases;" These are promises from the God who *cannot* lie! Hebrews 6:18. Truly He is faithful!

6

My Error, Not God's

When Lu'anna finished her Navy enlistment, she married Kenneth Daniels. He was, and is, not only a fine husband and father, but everything a mother-in-law could ask. Kenneth helped me move to San Diego, California in 1977.

As usual, I had fasted and prayed to find God's will. It seemed to me He said, "Go to San Diego!" Because Dad and I had become extraordinarily close, leaving him in Cape Cod was difficult. I was terribly homesick for him as we traveled westward. Satan kept whispering, "If this move was of God, you would not feel so bad!" I thought it was just my own thoughts. Christians often make that mistake. Like them, I listened! The Bible says he is "subtle," and we are often foolish.

Though aware of all that I allowed frets into my head. Perhaps it wasn't God's will! If I were going on my own, things would not work out as expected. As we were ready to cross from Nevada into California, I could not ask Kenneth to turn around and go back!

Suddenly, near Las Vegas something appeared on a mountain. As Kenneth never saw it, I must have had another vision. Whatever, the Face of Jesus was plainly there. One Hand reached out to me as He said, "I'm with you all the way!" - Oh, the blessing! God had confirmed the move west as really His will! I can recall that vision today, and the blessing returns to my spirit. Praise God for caring about His children, and doing something to help in times of need!

I soon found work at Hillcrest Receiving Home in San Diego. Children of all ages were cared for there. Lu'anna and Kenneth kindly let me live with them for a year. Like my girls, he is always "there" when I have a need. All four are generous with both time and money, and very supportive of this ministry. It is difficult to put into words how much I appreciate and love them. Lu'anna and Kenneth had three children by then: Tiffany, Kalisha, and Kenneth, Jr. Adding me to the family could not have been easy! Yet I never felt unwelcome.

Through Lu'anna I became involved in St. Stephens Church of God in Christ. I soon felt at home there, but my life took a drastic turn. A minister at St. Stephens seemed a humble man and greatly anointed. For some time I had been asking God for a husband filled with the Holy Spirit and sanctified to Him. Soon I began to "feel" that man was the answer to my prayer. The Lord has since reminded me that I did not ask Him specifically if that were true.

I counsel others, "You need only ask wisdom to receive it." Unfortunately, that good advice was ignored! Not for the first time, my "Feelings" were allowed to rule, instead of the Holy Spirit. Like a child wanting to cross the busy street alone, we opt to do something "ourself". God then removes His hand from the steering wheel of our lives, and lets us do our own thing.

As there are only two choices, self will put Satan at the wheel. Every Christian has learned bitter lessons that way, and I am not exception. Through His people and their prayers, God walked me down the path I chose. Like we who are parents, He loves the child, if not the rebellion.

When we married in 1978, Joann refused to live in his house. I was heartsick when she moved back to Connecticut to live with my sister, Loretta. Only fourteen years old, she saw that man more clearly than did I. We adults should listen more often to our children. If Jesus is Lord, their vision can be clearer. Too often an adult's vision is clouded by circumstances.

My new husband proved to be insanely jealous – of women friends or of men I barely knew. He was dictatorial and insisted I cease being an evangelist. That I could have accepted, if allowed to help in his own ministry. He forbade that, too, which made me feel totally useless. An evangelist's heart yearns to be about the Lord's business – saving souls! For the first time in years, I wasn't working for Him. That hurt!

Becky, eleven, could do nothing to please him. She usually stayed with other people because of his bitterness. That put guilt on me. Joe Brown, her real father, had always rejected Becky, and it was happening again. (Joe was trying to make amends for those early years, but her wounds weren't healed.) My marriage was outside God's will. As usually happens, I had difficulty in all areas. Too often loved ones get hurt when ' self makes choices. When we ignore His claim on our lives.'

When she reached sixteen, he threw her out of the house. I was desperately trying to make a go of the marriage, thinking it was ordained of God. Things speedily went from bad to worse. Once again I lived a tortured existence. My husband often talked of death. He swung from deep depression to where I was not allowed to follow.

Later, I learned from his first wife that the man was always moody. They were married twenty years. She said there was no peace in their home, as there was none in ours. Only Jesus brought any to my heart. God really worked in all that mess through my three stepchildren. They have always seemed to like me and we are friends today.

God had said long before that I was going to be an evangelist. The new man in my life not only rejected my ministry. He totally refuted God's claim on my life. Having heard nothing about all that before the marriage, it was difficult to believe. Those not called of God in a special way cannot relate to the situation.

I had been used by Him in so many ways, for many years. Souls had been saved, lives turned around, and miracles performed. For me to cease being an evangelist was impossible. The situation was very painful. Others could not comprehend the agony of losing a ministry which meant everything to me.

In 1983 my husband and I opened a food catering business. It was highly successful. Food prepared by others was delivered on trucks to different businesses. Car dealers, construction sites, and even beauty parlors were among our customers. Soon the Lord opened doors for us to take meals to the resit stop at Oceanside. That was a material blessing, both to us and to the church. We gave away meals if people were unable to pay, and God honored that. He touched lives through me during that time. I was blessed, as were many others.

I spent long hours at the rest stop, and prayed with those , who had needs. It was had work, both physically and emotionally exhausting. My husband couldn't see himself ministering out there. Part of my witness was handing out tracts. The same people came day after day – especially truck drivers.

One drug addict was delivered instantly as I prayed with him. He returned later, testifying to the Glory of God. Several without jobs asked prayer that they might be able to find one. Often somebody returned to report that God had been faithful, - and they were employed. Now and then money was offered me, for some did not understand. Refusing it, I explained we are only vesels through whom the Holy Ghost moves.

Paul wrote, in Ephesians 4:11, "Apostles, prophets, evangelists, as well as pastors and teachers, were given to the Body of Christ, which is His church. V. 12 explains that they were given for the "perfecting of the saints, for the work of the ministry, for the edifying of the body of Christ!"

Month after month my husband absolutely refused to believe that any woman could be an Evangelist. As my ordination was from God, being able to minister only at the rest stop proved something was very wrong. I knew there had been a misstep, but it was not clarified by the Holy Spirit for a while. Nothing is nothing worse for one committed to God than that.

Why did I put up with it for so long? Partly because I thought the Lord had put us together. To some that sounds peculiar, but the marriage vows were binding to me. Also, I had received no specific direction from the Holy Spirit, so I could not leave. An essential requirement for any evangelist is learning to wait on His instructions. Any Christian gets into trouble running ahead of God. For those called to be an evangelist, it is disastrous – as my situation proved!

Isaiah 61:1-3, Amplified, "The Spirit of the Lord God is upon me because the Lord has anointed and qualified me to preach the gospel of good tidings to the meek, the poor and afflicted. He has sent me to bind up and heal the broken-hearted, to proclaim liberty to the (physical and spiritual) captives and the opening of the prison and of the eyes to those who are bound; To proclaim the acceptable year of the Lord – the year for His favor – and the day of vengeance of our God; to comfort all who mourn;"

Though Isaiah and prophecying the ministry of Jesus -. Christ, my life was long ago committed to just what that says. Those called of God see that as their marching orders. When ministering in prisons, I feel deep compassion for those who are bound. Many of them, receiving Christ as personal Saviour, have been set free from death and destruction. Others are healed of sickness and disease. Statistics prove most of the inmates who receive Christ in prison leave forever. (Though some go back to minister in His Name.) Those who leave through other routes have a high rate of return. Evangelist McDonald was right on, God IS the Answer!

I was being taught a hard lesson. While walking through the valley of discouragement and depression, we look for someone to blame. Anyone will do — except ourselves! There was no forgiveness in my heart toward that new husband.

How easily we forget God's standard! Over and over and over Jesus taught about forgiveness. Matthew 6:14, KJV, "For if ye forgive men their trespasses, your heavenly Father will also forgive you: But if ye forgive not men their trespasses, neither will your Father forgive your trespasses."

How much plainer could it be? Peter asked Jesus in Matthew 18:21 how often they were to forgive, perhaps seven times? In V. 22, our Lord replied, "I say not unto thee, Until seven times, but, until seventy times seven." KJV

Jesus wants us to be loving wives, no matter what the situation. Frustrated at not being able to work for the Lord, I often failed in that area. The rest stop had to be catered seven days a week, twenty-four hours a day. It wasn't unusual for me to spend sixteen hours at a time. Of course, that meant coming home exhausted. Had there been any tenderness or compassion writing, I might have handled it differently. Physical work has always been therapeutic for me. But the strain of my husband's criticism, suspicions, and rejection was unbearable!

Feeling near a breakdown, I could feel the saints of God praying. Only a few knew what was going on in our home. Praise God, some were willing to listen and love me, no matter how difficult I was. A marriage speedily falling apart added to the strain of my full schedule. I found peace only in prayer.

It was discouraging to see Satan working, and be unable to stop him. Anything my spouse heard about me, he believed. Some of his friends' stories were outlandish! At the same time he was trying to chase away those who loved me. His anger, ever at the boiling point, drove him to senseless actions. One day he jerked the telephone out of the wall in a rage. After all, I might have received some comfort through it!

Today, having ministered to Spirit-filled Christians who suffer oppression, I see more clearly. At the time, I didn't recognize Satan's power over him. Disappointed by every aspect of the marriage, I failed to discern the problem. Not that he would have allowed me, or anyone else to minister! Long before I had been taught to "love the sinner while hating the sin." That seemed impossible concerning my spouse. Disappointment, like anything else negative, clouds our spiritual vision. The man was seen as the enemy, instead of Satan.

One of the most difficult things to bear was his anger when I served a guest food or drink. Coming from a close and hospitable family, I found that shocking. He deeply resented giving, in any form, perhaps because of his own deprived childhood. Never having received love, there was none for him to give.

As most people saw him as a minister of the gospel, I wondered if I were insane. A few, more aware of the true situation, were standing against the powers of evil in my behalf. How those praying friends were appreciated!

Evangelist Tony Young, a special sister in Christ, never failed to come when I needed her. Overseers of God's Helping Hand ministries in San Diego, she is never too busy to pray. Sister Tony is an anointed and beautiful person whom I love deeply. Unlike me, her discernment worked like radar!

Others at God's Helping Hand held me up in prayer. Mother Shepherd was especially dear, and I leaned upon her strength. Such a quiet woman, but her words always blessed me! When there seemed no hope, my spirit left her presence strengthened and knowing God was still on His Throne!

Trying to list names is risky, for someone is always missed. Two women especially blessed me – Betty Timbrook and Irene Powers. There were many others who called, prayed, and counseled. God responded by finding jobs to occupy that mind under siege. Working with the 700 Club on my day off helped immeasurably. I counseled and prayed for others by telephone, yet my own life was a shambles!

It was a great privilege to pray for those in need of help. Most of the young people calling into the 700 Club were depressed and even suicidal. Many of them were lonely," *felt unloved and didn't know where to turn. They went for anything which offered satisfaction -- drugs, alcohol, or sex. Instead, they found heartache and trouble!

It was really love they sought. Too many felt their parents cared nothing about them. Mothers and fathers trying to prove love with money or gifts always miss it. Most children yearn for their time and attention. My heart ached for those young people. Too many thought they were of no value, and called themselves "Throwaways."

We counselors told them about Jesus and about His love. Some did accept Him as Saviour. We tried to send them to a church or group that could minister to them. Of course, this was not always successful. Helping them helped me, for I desperately needed to think about something other than my own troubles.

We explained that God is love, I John 4:8, 16. Jesus said He and the Father were one, John 14:10, 11. A person can feel unloved, but the best solution to any problem is finding Him as Saviour and Lord. Jesus is the answer to questing souls and food for hungry hearts.

We are saved and filled with the Holy Spirit for a reason. God gives us power to battle Satan, not to attend church once or twice a week. The devil knows all about God's power. His strongholds have gone down before it time and time again. He sees us trying to help somebody without God's authority, and laughs. Wouldn't you, if a person tried to move a car, but never turned the key? Satan has no reason to fear the Christian who uses neither pray nor the Name of Jesus. He is perfectly safe when Bibles collect dust instead of being polished Swords!

Why do so many Spirit-filled people prefer helplessness to conquering evil? Why impotence when all of God's Power is waiting to be used? Perhaps because of fear – of failing, or fear of seeming odd. Or it may be lack of teaching. Many churches fail to instruct their people about the battle raging between Satan's realm and God's realm.

In the midst of all the turmoil in my life. Dad was fighting lung cancer in Massachusetts. I went back often as possible, though watching him suffer tore my heart. My husband tried to stop me, insisting it was a waste of money. That made no difference. I told him, "After all, I have only one father!"

Though he rejected my help for his ministry, many women were calling on the telephone who refused to leave a name. He explained it was all part of his ministry, yet he was VERY secretive. If I answered, he would jerk the phone from me and he would talk.

Obviously, things were not as I was being told, but what must I do? Though people suggested divorce, the Lord had not said this. My husband's cruelty, both physical and psychological, kept me constantly in prayer. I fasted often. Yet God would not let me leave. Not yet.

Earlier Irene Powers had introduced me to Home Ministry Fellowship in San Diego. How those people blessed me! I feel Charles Stilwell, president, is my spiritual father. A great man of God, he is anointed, dedicated, and truly loves the Lord. Reverend Stilwell is a man of wisdom and compassion. No matter how busy he is, he finds time for those in need. His wife, Bobbie, is also available, day or night. An anointed teacher, she has many areas of ministry.

As Dad's condition worsened, I went to spend a month with him and Mom in December of 1984. He and I talked about the Lord and prayed together. I have peace about his salvation. As he grew weaker, he knew his time on this earth was short. I, who had seen so many healed, expected a miracle. When he got no better, I flew home with a troubled heart. Didn't God care that a wonderful man was slipping away.,

I prayed, "Father, why can't Dad stay to enjoy his salvation?" It seemed unfair, for I had long anticipated is being involved in my ministry. The Lord had touched so many through my prayers, it was frustrating not to get the response I desperately wanted. For so long, I had heard from God, but He was silent. Bitterly disappointed, I began to question His love.

The problem wasn't God's refusing to speak, but my refusal to listen! Why? Perhaps fearing He might say what I didn't want to hear? Communication with the Lord cannot be emphasized enough! Prayer was not meant to be a one-way conversation. Too many pray "Gimme, gimme," as if the Heavenly Father were Santa.

I've noticed people think it is important to communicate with others, yet never wait while the Holy Spirit talks. Some ask how one hears from God. It can be through His Word. Often He gives encouragement without specifically replying. It can be a "knowing" inside our hearts about what He wants. Gospel music has often ministered to me. In fact, I was healed through it once. It can be prophecy or a word of knowledge, through another believer. God loves to use little children, and that can be disconcerting. They have a freshness about them and are more open to receive than are adults.

Disappointed that Dad wasn't improving, and watching a marriage disintegrate before my eyes, I grew unhappy with God. No one has any right to question the Creator, and it cost me His joy. My depression worsened, until I found it difficult to minister at all.

Constantly thinking about Dad, I wasn't aware what was happening at home. In the midst of such trauma I believed the marriage was God's divine plan. Expecting the Lord to heal our relationship, I was not prepared to hear, "I want a divorce!"

Eventually I understood. Another woman had entered the picture, so my husband wanted out. His decision took the burden off my own shoulders, but anyone walking that path knows about guilt. It is laid heavily upon us by the legalistic members of the church.

Those committed to Jesus know divorce is not His perfect will. But people who never walked that path should be careful not to judge! Only sisters and brothers in the Lord who have can relate to the pain. One is devastated at so many levels! We put guilt upon ourselves, thinking ours the sin when a marriage fails. We do not need it added by fellow believers!

Discouragement eats at one's soul, for Satan uses it to scream, "Failure! You failed as a wife – or husband!" Rejection is one of his better tools, and it grows sharper as he uses it. Of course, the pain is greater if we've failed in that area more than once!

If you know someone involved in the funeral of a marriage, go to him or her. Absolutely refuse to listen to the gossips. Remind those who are tearing down a reputation to "think on" good things about the people involved. Offer a shoulder upon which to cry – or listen. People in pain need understanding silence more than advice!

Use Matthew 7:1, 2 for your edification and that of others. "Do not judge and criticize and condemn others, so that you may not be judged and criticized and condemned yourselves. For just as you judge and criticize and condemn others you will be judged and criticized and condemned, and in accordance with the measure you deal out to others, it will be dealt out again to you. (Amplified Bible, emphasis my own.)

That should keep some of the Body of Christ on their knees for a while! Remember, divorce can happen to anybody. Love someone through it and one day YOU may reap the benefits. It is of epidemic proportions everywhere, even in the Body of Christ. There is no guarantee you won't be next!

If there is any virtue to divorce, it must be through forcing us to our knees. I attempted going it alone, without Jesus, as others have tried. Often, hurt or angry, we move away – cease praying – but He never moves at all! We soon learn He's easiest found from a kneeling position!

Jesus patiently waits for us to humble ourselves, to admit that He really is the answer! Satan knows exactly how to tempt believers. And he *can* alleviate the pain. Unfortunately sin is the only medicine in his bag. To some it's sex, to some alcohol, and to some, like me, he offers unforgiving anger. Whatever, temptation, is never sin. No, but the giving in to it is, for that separates us from God.

Jesus patiently waits for us to humble ourselves, to admit that He really is the answer! Satan knows exactly how to tempt believers. And he *can* alleviate the pain. Unfortunately sin is the only medicine in his bag. To some it's sex, to some alcohol, and to some, like me, he offers unforgiving anger. Whatever, temptation, is never sin. No, but the giving in to it is, for that separates us from God.

To those born again and filled with the Holy Ghost, all Heaven's power is available. They need only stand fast. Christians who love someone who is hurting must pray while battling Satan in his or her behalf. Many in the Church do neither. Instead they judge, and automatically slide into sin!

If the divorced person succumbs to Satan, there is always a way back to God. My own sin was unforgiveness. Sometimes people miss a blessing in not letting Jesus love through them. How grateful I was for those who never waivered. Who offered shoulders and not judgmental wisdom! To so many I am indebted beyond description.

My husband's daughter blessed me over and over. As she never seemed a "step" daughter, we don't use that word. I love her as much as my own flesh and blood. By my side through it all, she offered much prayer and encouragement. When things looked darkest, she was there ministering to me. Her husband and their sons are also very precious to me.

God has so blessed me through daughters. It has not been easy for Lu'anna, Joann, and Becky to understand my committment to the work God called me to do. They know and love Him, but often they must have seen the Lord as an interloper. Children of other evangelists will relate, for our time is not our own. My girls have never deprived me by withholding of themselves in the emotional realm or in the material. Praise God! How thankful I am for them all.

7

Back In God's Will

During and after the divorce Satan offered me his bitter fruit. Like Eve, I "took of the fruit thereof and did eat." Galatians 5:19-21 KJV, lists these as "the works of the flesh." I found myself full of hatred, wrath, and strife. Unforgiveness joined that motley crew, bringing with it discouragement, guilt, and a sense of failure. God's fruit, verses 22 and 23, start with Love, Joy and Peace. Those called by Him to a special ministry are as human as anyone else. Of course, standing up there preaching, they are more visible. People watch us to see if our lives reflect our preaching.

I found the way back to His Peace, just as anyone can. Friends offered compassion and love. Refusing to judge, they helped me along the way. Jesus said, Matthew 5:14, NIV, "You are the light of the world." V. 16, "let your light so shine before men." Those precious people, like beacons, lit the way for me. And Jesus was there, waiting, nail-scarred hands full of forgiveness. Those hands always hold the antidote to what Satan offers.

After the divorce a precious friend, Marcia Garcia, and I decided to visit the Stilwells. They had moved the ministry to southeastern Arizona a few years earlier. Typically Charles and Bobbie insisted we stay at their Retreat House. Hank and Irene Powers were running it for Home Ministry Fellowship, at the time. Bathed in the love of all those dear people, my wounds began to heal.

From the Cross Jesus said, "Father, forgive them, for they know not what they do," When we learn how to forgive those who have done us wrong – forgive His way – God can begin the healing. Though it was filed in my memory, I had misplaced Matthew 5:43 and 44 NIV. Jesus speaking, "You have heard that it was said, you shall love your

53

neighbor and hate your enemy. But I tell you, Love your enemies and pray for those who persecute you."

Jesus taught many deep truths there on the mountain. Easiest to ignore is that one. We are willing to love our neighbors as ourselves, or at least to give it lip service. But everybody knows it's impractical to love an enemy. He may retaliate by kicking in your teeth! Nobody expects us to love enemies, Nobody except Jesus! If we want Him to be our Lord, that is the criterion. We are to love, not hate, those who "deserve" to be hated.

Forgiving "seventy times seven" was not what I wanted to hear. My ex-husband continued to persecute me financially. He did everything possible to make my life difficult. Forgiveness seemed impossible! Like those to whom Jesus spoke almost two thousand years ago, I could not understand. How does one forgive time after time? That isn't natural. For the human heart, it is inconceivable.

Yet Jesus had said I must forgive the man who nearly ruined my mind and tried to destroy my ministry. I could not, but the Christ within me found it easy! When this Evangelist knelt to admit the anger and hate, He did the forgiving. Once I knelt to admit MY sin, supernaturally it left. Hallelujah, praise the name of Jesus! All the bitter fruit disappeared. Satan offers it to me, from time to time, but I know better now. It gets easier and easier to reject. Jesus never, ever, asks for something we cannot give. He was tempted in all ways.

Healing cannot begin until we forgive. It alone opens the door locked by hate. Once it is open, His love floods in to wash away Satan's fruit from our hearts. The world cannot comprehend, but it happens. Praise God, it happens!

Today it would be impossible to hate my former husband. He still thinks of ways to make my life difficult. The man who caused me so much pain suffered greatly as a child. How could I not forgive him? Satan knows Jesus will soon return. Because his days are numbered, he fights a desperate battle. He is the source of the child abuse which is a horror across our land. Satan, not the man I married, was the true enemy!

Once more, the Lord said, "Time to move." In August of 1985 I felt led to buy a home in Arizona. God's plan wasn't clear, but I knew He wanted me there. For how long, or doing what, I had no idea. The house out in the country, and lonely. My zip code and Stilwells were the same, but our homes miles apart.

In San Diego there had been a host of friends near. Not only were they further apart in Arizona, but people seemed busier. I felt like the Israelites did when sent into the wilderness. Looking back, however, I realize the "wilderness experience" was already behind me.

Praise God, a time of service had come. The Lord has always moved in "mysterious ways" in my life. Again there was a ministry waiting. When the Holy Ghost said, "Go back into the prisons," I remembered that lesson at Sing Sing. Approaching the Chaplain at Douglas State Prison, I asked about ministering there. What "unspeakable joy" to find Keith Poweley, as Chaplain. He is a Spirit-filled man, and on fire for God! Many convicts had come to the Lord under his shepherding, so the ground was prepared for me to work there.

Several others came to Jesus as Saviour and some were filled with the Holy Spirit. I was particularly blessed by people the Lord had accompany me into the prisons. Of course, sometimes it was necessary to go alone. Both prisons were far from Sunizona, which meant miles of travel, but I could not complain. It was heaven to feel back in the Lord's will.

In both prisons there was a real hunger for the Word of God. I taught Bible Studies and was blessed as men grew in the Lord. One of my life's highlights was found "behind the wall." A young inmate suggested the Christians in Douglas Prison make a tape for me. They sang beautifully and he preached a great message. On it they put words of appreciation about my ministry. I will always cherish that tape.

Kitty Preas and I met at a Joy Fellowship meeting soon after God began to use me at Douglas Prison. She was acquainted at Fort Grant, a minimum security prison north of Wilcox, Arizona. We were so blessed by the men there. Kitty ministers beautifully, singing and playing. When her little daughter, Becky, went along those inmates were especially pleased. Kitty's music is anointed, and Becky was a blessing to men away from their own children.

Another new friend, Joyce Mounts, accompanied me often. Stilwells and Powers also went with me from time to time. They all found joy inside those bleak walls, as I so often have.

Being incarcerated is hard on marriages. The spouse can see no future to that relationship. Usually there is no money with which to travel and few write. I remember a quite young inmate whose wife had written she never wanted to see him again. After we prayed together, and he forgave her, that lady changed. She began reading her Bible and promised to visit as soon as possible.

Another whose marriage was in trouble was the Chaplain's clerk. He had a long sentence but after our prayer, decided to believe for an early release. She joined with him in prayer and believing for it. They both saw God's Hand in that miracle. At last report that couple was continuing to work for the Lord.

During the summer of 1986 my own Becky went into both prisons with me. Could she ever "rap" with those men! They loved her and seemed very open to what she said. That experience helped swing her toward the Lord's direction in her own life.

In Arizona, once I truly repented. Dad's death was easier to handle. God in His wisdom knew my father had always ministered to others. Though I was frustrated and disappointed that he wasn't healed, the Lord gave me new insights. My father had always loved people and often helped the needy. I often hear, "What a good man your father was!" No one ever spoke unkindly of him, to my knowledge. Albert Joseph lived the life Christ taught, loyal, dedicated, and compassionate. I never knew him to lie, and he was honest. Dad had an humble quality we seldom see, and was never comfortable being praised.

When the Lord showed me all this, I rejoiced. The disappointment about his not being involved in my ministry faded away. It always does when we pray, repent, and ask forgiveness. His was a different work than I had expected, but the Lord used him. In my spirit I am convinced that fine man is in Kingdom Land. All my doubts and fears are gone. The Lord is good and "His mercy endureth forever." Psalm 136, KJV.

Much about life we cannot comprehend. One day I shall ask the Lord all those unanswered questions. I believe He will gladly reply, for the Holy Spirit often reveals answers to me. Don't misunderstand! There are times when none is forthcoming. Experience has shown that God is putting something together then, which my vision is too limited to see. We need to reject frets, seek His will above all else, and wait with expectation for Him to move.

That "above all else" must especially include our own will. If we force ourselves to lay it at the foot of the Cross, God is free to do what He wants with us.

An Evangelist must "tune in" to God, ignoring other voices. With the best of intentions, man offers advice that may not be from the Holy Spirit. One called to minister must listen and obey Him whether people understand or not. I have been through persecutions because of that. I must walk His way, no matter the cost. People sometimes think – that I feel superior – but my Lord knows the truth.

During one trip to Ft. Grant a young man identified himself as Muslim. He definitely did not believe Jesus Christ was God. Later, alone with me, he received Him as Saviour. It was such joy to have that man faithfully attend Bible studies and grow in the Lord.

I prayed with the men about their smoking. Several were delivered. It is always exciting to see God move, but I feel compassion for those in prison. They have so little pleasure, it takes real dedication to let God take away any habit.

I believe strongly in prophecy and I am often used that way. It is necessary, though, to be wary. Satan can use well-intentioned people, and he does. Jesus said that would happen in Matthew 24:11. Peter wrote, under the unction of the Holy Spirit, "But also (in those days) there arose false prophets among the people, just as there will be false teachers among yourselves, who will subtly and stealthily introduce heretical doctrines – destructive heresies – even denying and disowning the Master who bought them, bringing upon themselves swift destruction." II Peter 2:1, Amp.

I try to always examine the prophecy and "try the spirits." If it is not of God, it must be ignored. John 4:1-3. If it is, our spirits should receive the witness.

Too often Christians run about wanting a prophecy. They seek a "message," instead of the Messenger Himself! The best way to get such a word from God is on your knees, praying and waiting for Him to reply. Sometimes a fast is necessary. If led by God to fast, whether one or more days, direction will come. The blessing is so much greater when it comes directly to us. God never makes a mistake! Man may be confused in the flesh, or not hearing accurately from the Holy Spirit. Words may be coming from the wrong source. Satan's messages lead only to sorrow.

It is imperative we test the spirit as prophecy comes forth. When false it has destroyed marriages, torn families apart, and caused Believers to make wrong decisions. Even churches have been split by messages not from God. Speaking as from Him but not by His Spirit is a dangerous thing.

I've seen beautiful Spirit-filled people lose their joy or their peace, because they did not seek God for themselves. Others have backslidden because of a wrong message. One who pulls a soul back into the hands of Satan pays a dear price. We all need to look to Jesus for His guidance and understanding. "In all our ways we must acknowledge God, and He will direct our paths." Proverbs 3:6.

Jesus can be anything in your life – doctor, lawyer, whatever you need. When all others disappear. He will be a friend. He can be a husband if there isn't one, or parent. He has been all these and more to me!

Often it was for sex sins the men wanted deliverance. So much evil flourishes in a prison atmosphere. Homosexuality is rampant. That law of the jungle rules – the weak must bow to the strong. People on the "outside" cannot comprehend what courage it takes to become a Christian there. Other inmates see any man who decides that fighting is wrong as "weak." I did a lot of praying and fasting for new converts. Once that new Babe in Christ learns about God's power, he can let it fight any battles.

There were a number of black inmates at Ft. Grant. They seemed to especially appreciate my ministry. As I did theirs, for in Southeastern Arizona we are few and far between!

It is wonderful to know our Lord shows no partiality – Romans 2:11 Amplified Bible – "For God shows no partiality (undue favor, or unfairness; with Him one man is not different from another)." Hallelujah! He loves us, black man, white, or yellow. He sees them all the same. Jesus Christ doesn't ask if you are Catholic, Baptist, Jewish, or nothing at all! He cares not from whence you came, only about your final destination. He died that the world might be saved. John 3:16. It was for sinners He left mansions in Heaven to die on a Roman Cross!

The greatest of all miracles is salvation. Yes, beyond healing blind eyes or making the lame walk, salvation is the miracle of miracles. When God washes a sinner in that precious Blood – forgiving all his sins never to remember them again – it is truly beyond human comprehension. He cleans us up and writes our names in the Lamb's Book of Life. Praise God! Revelation 21:27.

With the world as it is, I don't know how anyone can survive without Christ. People use the word "Christian" carelessly today. It bothers me when some claim to belong to Him, yet know little about what that means. Originally it was used to identify those who followed Jesus Christ. True Christians not only accepted Him as Saviour, but also want to live as He did – to love as He did. The streets of our world are crowded, but not with people like that! It means living a Christ-centered life. It means keeping ourselves unspotted by the world, its thoughts, attitudes, and activities.

When first saved, I thought "born-again" meant no more suffering. It was soon clear that growing in the Lord meant pain. To reign with Christ we must suffer as He did.

II Timothy 2:12. Why? Suffering accomplishes at least two things. It forces our minds to see that He alone can help. (When things go well, we decide God isn't necessary.) Second, as gold is refined in the furnace, the dross is purged from us. Isaiah 1:25, KJV.

I never tell anyone the consecrated life will be easy. However, God's Word promises He won't put on us more than we can endure. I Corinthians 10:13. Also Psalm 46:1 says He will be our help in times of trouble. To claim those and other promises, we must keep our eyes on Him and not allow the world and its idols to replace the Lord. Exodus 20:5.

Yes, Shirley Home is a Jesus-fanatic! Worse has been said, but it doesn't bother me, for I know the Word! Jesus, being divine, finds nothing impossible. When bills pile up, unfailingly He provides money.

Prayer is the solution. If we but call out, He replies, though not always as expected. When there seems to be no answer, God may be saying, "Wait!" He always replies on His schedule, not on mine. The Lord knows what is best for any servant. Leaving it to Him often means a bigger blessing than expected. I've often said, "Don't box God in, He may want to do more than that."

Two couples, dear friends of mine, were praying for now homes. All four wanted *His perfect will.* One pair knew their home would be used for a church, the other did not. Believing that God *would* provide, both presented petitions to Him, and left them there. Satan offered worries, but those were rejected. Having decided they wanted God to make all the decisions, no matter what that might mean, neither fretted about the future home. It was His to supply, and to use as He saw fit. Their part was to do whatever He led them to do.

God was faithful – you never saw two more beautiful double-wide mobile homes! They are similar, but perfectly arranged for each need. One held seventy people when dedicated as a church. Both have been used for healing meetings, prison ministry, potlucks, or whatever else might bless the Body of Christ. Now the second one is also a church, of course, God knew all the time that it would be. No one else even suspected such a thing!

Those are only two examples of God's provision. His warehouse is limitless and His love even greater. What you *think* you need may be tiny in comparison to what God wants you to have. He loves to bless His own, and to surprise them!

With such power available, isn't it sad that prayer is no longer popular in our country as it once was? In homes, churches, and other meetings it often lies idle. It has been banished from the schools. Man has replaced prayer with programs, entertainments, seminars – even social gatherings. Almost anything will draw a crowd except a prayer meeting! The Bible says in I Thessalonians 5:17 we are to "pray without ceasing." I thank God for those groups – small or large – across American continuing to meet only for prayer. They meet and expect God to move, and He does!

The Holy Ghost often wakes me at odd hours, saying, "Pray!" Usually He doesn't explain why. As Paul taught in Ephesians 6:18, I pray in the Spirit language until told to stop. If some person comes to mind, or a particular situation, I pray accordingly. At other times He has me fast and pray for a specific need – deliverance, healing, or whatever.

Occasionally He reveals something which needs prayer in a dream or a vision. One time I "saw" my daughter, Becky, covered with blood. She was in a New York City school at the time, and I realized she was crying. I wakened trembling all over, for she looked terrible. Aware she was in trouble, I began to pray and continued all day, asking God to keep her safe.

Soon afterwards Becky called. "My father got me so upset it almost caused me to have a nervous breakdown," she said. "The devil kept saying, 'kill yourself!' Instead, I went to a Spirit-filled church and asked for prayer." At that exact time I had been on my knees praying for her. Praise God, "the effectual fervent prayer of a righteous man availeth much!" James 5:16, KJV. Jesus is our righteousness – I Corinthians 1:30.

I was thankful Becky went to a Spirit-filled church, for those people usually know about the power that Jesus left us. The Gifts of the Spirit are His way of manifesting Himself in the church, yet they can cause one group of members to turn against the other. If prophecy, speaking in tongues, interpretations, etc. are in evidence, that church should "be aglow and burning with the Spirit."

Too often ignorance of the Bible is the problem. God's Word has not been studied to find what it says about the gifts. Paul wrote about them over and over. If God truly is living and not dead, shouldn't we expect His Church to be more than a social club? More than a place to spend one hour every Sunday morning, whether or not we are growing?

Daily we sin – hourly in some cases – and daily we need to repent. If there seems no need of repentance in my life, I had better rush to kneel at the Cross! Immediately I must ask Jesus to forgive that arrogance and pride! One of the signs of TRUE Salvation is our seeing sin as it is. (And seeing it *in us first!*) It may be sin of thoughts, words, or of actions. Whatever, repentance must come from a sincere and humble heart. God who sees the heart immediately recognizes hypocrisy – I Samuel 16:7. A "broken and contrite heart He will not despise – Isaiah 51:17.

If a tiny flicker enters our minds saying, "You are righteous because of good works," or "Your walk is purer than" somebody else's, then it must be recognized at once as evil. Such flickers are danger signals! We must quickly ask forgiveness. Failure to do that causes the flicker to become a flame and soon it will consume us. That is idolatry at its worst. Satan delights in helping us put ourselves on a pedestal. Why? As we kneel to worship ourselves, we pay homage to his most loyal slaves! Self knows only one master, and rejects anything not from Satan. Though self may *think* he's in control, the devil is pulling the strings.

When Jesus is rejected as Lord, only one choice remains – Satan! Putting the devil in charge means his demons are in control. What does God's Word say about "works of the flesh" in Galatians 5:19-21? Immorality, idolatry, jealousy, and anger, to name only a few. It is a mystery to me why people choose the kingdom of darkness over the Kingdom of Light. The flesh over the "fruit of the Spirit," which is also listed in galatians 5. Paul wrote, in Hebrews 1:14 Amp. "Are not the angels all (servants) ministering spirits, sent out in the service of God for the assistance of those who are to inherit salvation?

If only Christians would spend more time in prayer and fasting. Seeking God, not worrying, results in miracles. In their own lives as well as others. A loved one's safety can depend on those "fervent" prayers. Especially for one who doesn't know Jesus.

Most Christians have at one time or another felt God's Hand of protection. Haven't you heard, or said, "My guardian angel held that car from hitting us?" Or "It had to be an angel helping that child, he wasn't even hurt!" No true believer doubts that God's "ministering spirits" are sent to serve those who are heirs of Christ's salvation.

People of the world, who know little of Jesus and His love, cannot relate to that supernatural protection. We who walk in it are astounded to see what God can do!

My trips to Arizona prisons covered miles of uninhabited desert. Though no people lived along those roads, there were skunks, coyotes, and rattlesnakes. Any one of them could petrify this city girl with fright! I had a few close calls, but was never forced to walk, for which God be praised!

Often my funds ran low. Living purely on faith can be traumatic, especially for one of an independent nature. One such night, driving home from Douglas Prison about ten-thirty, I saw a red light on the dash. To prove it meant "empty gas tank," my motor died.

Being in such a desolate spot, with only coyotes and snakes for company, was frightening. Not daring to get out and walk, I began to pray and cry out to God.

After about ten minutes the Holy Spirit said, "Turn the ignition on and press the gas pedal hard." As I obeyed, the motor roared to life. He then said, "Don't take your foot off that pedal until you get home!" For twenty miles I pressed that accelerator down, not lifting my foot. As the car turned in the driveway at home, it sputtered and died.

There have been many instances of divine protection or help through the years. Another time – returning from Douglas Prison alone – my lights went out. It was rare to see another car along that strip of highway, and houses are several miles apart. Wanting to panic, I pulled over to stop. Once God was asked to help, His faithfulness could be depended on!

The Holy Spirit said, "Open that little panel in the dashboard." Inside were several fuses. I said, "Lord, I don't know which one is which." That still small voice instructed me to take one out and replace it with a certain other one. The Holy Ghost knows everything. That includes how a car's electric system works. He was obeyed, and the lights came on immediately. I drove home, shouting praises to my Lord!

God had small groups scattered over the desert to which He wanted to minister. I was blessed by those wonderful sisters and brothers in Christ. Their generosity meant so much! I was given garden produce in summer and gifts from their freezers in winter. Invited to speak, I often spent the night on an outlying ranch. Such a totally new way of life, but the quiet and peace blessed my soul!

Young lives were turned around, while older ones matured. One meeting I particularly remember as exciting. While traveling toward it, I told myself, "What can God do at a Methodist church?" Well, it was proven once again that He is no "respecter of persons." During the altar call we had "wall to wall" people on the floor, slain in the Spirit. Some had never seen that manifestation of the Holy Ghost, but He was there in power.

The one-family band was talented as well as tuned-in to the Spirit. The beautiful young mother confided later, "I told God not to put me on the floor. After all, I teach these kids, that would never do!" Laughing with delight, she said, "He used me to minister among them. Then proceeded to slay you know who, and do the work needed!"

So often after ministering, I have to move on. It is the bane of an Evangelist's life. However, in Southeastern Arizona it was a privilege and joy to stay, watching people grow in the Lord. Hank and Irene Powers had been led into the ministry. They had long been precious friends. Their church people took this Evangelist to its heart. Again, the Lord used me and lives were changed. He is so good, and generous beyond measure with His Love!

Bobbie Stilwell and I waked up one morning with the same God-given idea. He wanted a Christian bookstore opened in the area. Home Ministry did the funding and they asked me to run it. What a beautiful opportunity to minister! We had Prayer meetings there often, as well as praying with individuals. It was a new facet of ministry, and I was blessed through it.

8

My Two Families

In whatever place the Lord calls me to minister, He gives me a spiritual family. In some, I found spiritual parents – Geraldine McDaniels, New York City and Reverend Stilwell, Sunizona, Arizona. I have been blessed through so many. In good times or bad ones, the Lord has always used His people to minister to Evangelist Shirley Home. How grateful I am! Many have given sacrificially from their purses. Others have given me a home and oh, the meals I've eaten prepared by the Body of Christ!

Across the United States, my spiritual relatives are a source of comfort and support. Many of them pray for me daily, and hear from God about needs in my life before I am aware they exist.

One time Sister Toni Young called me from San Diego. She knew my step son was being married soon, and about my very empty bank account. It was wonderful to hear her say, compassionately, "The Lord said you needed a new dress and shoes for the wedding, so I am sending them."

Times without number, the Lord has blessed me in such ways – through His people. Because not only do they prove their love, but they also prove His! I pray for this spiritual family often, and appreciate hearing that someone has been blessed afterwards.

There are many beautiful things about having Jesus as Lord. One of them, fellowship among believers, is a rare jewel indeed. It is totally incomprehensible to the unsaved. Even our earthly families cannot see what it is that makes us "closer than brothers." Jesus Christ and the Word are one – John 1:1 – and His Love is represente by that of His people.

The Bible speaks of individual believers as "members" of Christ's Body, of which He is "the Head." From that viewpoint, it matters not whether one is the foot and another the elbow, for each is equally important. Perhaps that explains the marvelous fellowship which is found nowhere else. Where the Body of Christ functions as it was intended, people love "in spite of" not because of. Whether theology disagrees is unimportant, it can be worked out. Ignoring different doctrines, age, or race, each sees the Saviour in the other. Nothing can break that bond, though Satan ever tries. The Church of Christ is made up of believers who stand fast on His being "Son of the Living God." That is called the Fellowship of the Saints, and brings delight unto the heart of God.

I thank Him for all my spiritual family because we can worship the Lord, play games, sing, or enjoy visiting. Always we pray for one another, whether together or apart. Perhaps that is the most precious of all His gifts – knowing if we ask for prayer it will be done as I Thessalonians 5:17 Amp. says, "perseveringly," praise God! We share things the world could never even discuss. We cry together, laugh together, eat or fast together. How beautiful it is that God builds us into families.

That is especially helpful for those with unsaved relatives. Once we find Jesus as Lord and Saviour, our families often reject us – or think we have rejected them! The more we strive to walk with Jesus, the more we seem "peculiar" – I Peter 2:9, KJV.

Once having found Him, our hearts yearn to share Him with those closest to us. Time after time He is rejected by those very people we love most. Sometimes it is the fault of that new convert, who comes across as "holier than thou," as if they had become instantly perfect. More often, it is due to unbelief. Whether doubting that God could save and change a member of the family, or doubting that God is real – our relatives often spurn the Gospel.

It is very important that we remember only the Holy Spirit can change hearts. It is our duty only to share Salvation with the lost. Only God converts the lost, because only He knows the condition of an individual heart. He sees into every closet and cupboard there, and can recognize a heart ready to admit the Master.

Most difficult of all to reach with the Gospel are the "good" people. Those who never used drugs, robbed anybody, or practiced adultery cannot see why they need saving. Their puzzled question is, "why do I need a Saviour, to save me from what?" Only God's Word will open those minds to His truth. Only His Spirit knows how to explain that

Jesus Christ is *the way* to eternal life with God. Man cannot convict another he is lost, but God's Word makes it very clear. John 3:16-18.

We are to pray and to believe as did Paul, when the Philippian jailer fell down before him, asking how to be saved. Acts 16:31 Amp, "Believe in and on the Lord Jesus Christ," Paul replied, "that is give yourself up to Him, take yourself out of your own keeping and entrust yourself into His keeping, and you will be saved; [and this applies both to] you and your household as well."

I believe Paul meant by "household" that our families would spent eternity with God. We have the right to claim their salvation, and to believe for it. God will do it if we but believe. Thousands of families have come to Him because one member refused to doubt, and totally trusted God to do what He said He would.

Of course, it's imperative unsaved people see Christ in the way we live. Love, joy, peace, patience, kindness, goodness, faithfulness, gentleness, and self-control have to show in us. Galatians 5:22-24 Amp When these "fruits of the Spirit," as Paul called them, manifest in our lives, family members see a change. They realize it has to be supernatural, and want what they see. It is not wise to preach at families, but to love and accept them where they are. Jesus did, and those walls came tumbling down.

This story began with three frightened, abandoned children. Today, the eldest, Shirley Home, is an evangelist with headquarters at Sunizona, Arizona. Her brother, Albert Joseph, lives in Sacramento. He is a serious man, but when smiling, his face lights up to become strikingly handsome. His son, Kevin, is really a Bible scholar. I prayed for my brother's salvation fifteen years, and now, praise God, that he found the Lord. Don't let Satan put discouragement on you about unsaved loved ones. Keep praying, and make yourself believe God's Word is true and He *is* listening.

Sister Diane, raised by Grandmother Roderick, is small and still looks like our mother. She inherited Grandmother's wonderful sense of humor. David and Michael, her twin boys, are well mannered, affectionate, and respectful. Both are in college and have jobs.

Loretta Towells is shorter, and shy. She has a pretty face, with helping those in need. Once Loretta becomes your friend, she is one forever. She and her daughters inherited their beautiful voices from Dad's family. They used to sing in the church choir. Loretta baby lives in New Haven, Connecticut.

Jackie died recently at the age of twenty-five. Though it was extremely painful to her family, I praise God that she received Christ when eleven while living with us in Larelton, New York. She used to sing Gospel music and was anointed to pray for the sick as well as in prophecy. Satan robbed her of God's gifts, and she followed him, listening to his lies.

Before Jackie died, she called me. "Aunt Shirley," she said, "I want to get back with the Lord." I believe she did, for there is a real peace in my heart about her.

Through all those years I kept her in prayer and believed God would answer. We must never put a time limit on Him.